UNDER THE VIADUCT

MEMORIES FROM THE MANOR AND BEYOND

UNDER THE VIADUCT

MEMORIES FROM THE MANOR AND BEYOND

DEBRA KAPLAN LOW

BOOK STREET
PRESS

Chandler, Arizona, USA

Linda F. Radke, Publisher
Book Street Press
An imprint of Story Monsters LLC
4696 W. Tyson St.
Chandler, AZ 85226–2903
480.940.8182
Publisher@storymonsters.com
www.BookStreetPress.com

Publisher's Cataloging-In-Publication Data

Names: Low, Debra Kaplan, author.
Title: Under the viaduct : memories from the Manor and beyond / by Debra Kaplan Low.
Description: Chandler, Arizona, USA : Book Street Press, [2021] | Includes bibliographical references.
Identifiers: ISBN 9781589852457 (paperback) | ISBN 9781589852471 (ebook)
Subjects: LCSH: Low, Debra Kaplan--Childhood and youth. | South Chicago (Chicago, Ill.)--Biography. | LCGFT: Autobiographies.
Classification: LCC F548.68.S68 L69 2021 (print) | LCC F548.68.S68 (ebook) | DDC 977.311092--dc23

Printed in the United States of America

Editor: Paul Howey
Cover Design: Kris Taft Miller
Set in Arno Pro by Raphaël Freeman MISTD, Renana Typesetting
Proofreaders: Ruthann Meyer, Cristy Bertini
Project Manager: Patti Crane

DEDICATION

Under the Viaduct is dedicated to my husband, Stuart Low, a continual source of love, wisdom, humor, kindness, inspiration, teasing, and good-natured "torture." I am blessed by Stu's enduring presence in my life. We recently celebrated the 51st anniversary of our first date.

I also dedicate this book to our only child, David Low. I have cherished David from his arrival as a newborn, through his development into a toddler, boy, and adult—and now as a husband to Katie and as an amazing father to their young daughter, Elizabeth (Ellie) Joy, and a newborn daughter, Alexandra (Lexie) Louise. I am proud of David for his many achievements but even more for his abundant kindness. I thank David for his honesty, egalitarian worldview, wise insights, and always for his love.

This book is also dedicated to the memory of my mother, Iris Stone Kaplan, the most loving, kind, and forgiving person I have ever known. My mother suffered many losses and indignities, yet she somehow maintained sweetness and optimism throughout her entire life. She was a role model to me in many ways, one of the best people I have ever known.

Finally, this book is dedicated to those who reside—and have resided—under the viaduct in the Manor.

Maybe the journey isn't so much about becoming anything.
Maybe it's about un-becoming everything that isn't really you,
so you can be who you were meant to be in the first place.

—Paulo Coelho

INTRODUCTION

*Every person from your past lives as a shadow in your mind. Good or bad, they
all helped you write the story of your life and shaped the person you are today.*

– Doe Zantamata

In Arizona, where I have lived since 1979, mountain ranges, foothills,
Indian reservations, rivers, and canals delineate municipalities,
neighborhoods, and social classes. In Chicago, it was the viaducts
that subdivided our little culturally intact neighborhoods. They were
built to accommodate freight tracks a block deep and miles long, but
they did far more than that. Where I grew up, viaducts separated our
area from the rest of Chicago, and in so doing, artificially served as
borders insulating the subcultures and attitudes of neighborhoods
in the city.

Under the Viaduct is the story of my life in Chicago's South Side
neighborhoods and beyond, focusing primarily on the Manor, the area
south of the 95th Street viaducts. My story will take you on a journey
through both sides of the viaduct, from the Windy City and into the
western Chicago "suburbs" of metropolitan Phoenix.

In these pages, you will meet imperfect families, quirky neighbors,
and questionable mentors. I will share my experiences with misogyny
and bigotry, ethnic and racial tensions, financial challenges, spiritual

journeys, life losses, and the environmental and sociological challenges affecting our community.

Some of the characters in this book are real people, while others are influenced by actual people and events. Some are exaggerated for comic relief. Other characters and stories are purely fictionalized, born in the murky darkness of my imagination. Some names are changed to protect the innocent and to spare the identities of the less-than-innocent.

Each of us views our world through our own unique lenses, however distorted they may be. This book is based on my personal stories and imaginings. It is not intended to be an all-encompassing story of life in the Manor. This is my story, and I hope you enjoy it.

Chapter One

Paradise was Found Under the Viaduct

I grew up with Marla, Stevie, Marky, and Nectarios, just off Route 41, under the longest, darkest, scariest viaducts you've ever seen. We didn't exactly live *under* the 95th Street viaducts, but we sure spent a lot of time in their shadow. If you wanted to get from almost anywhere in Chicago to our little neighborhood, you had to slow your car down at 94th Street and Jeffery, hold your breath, and pray you weren't driving behind a diesel-farting old CTA bus. If you got stuck behind a bus too many times in the viaduct, my friend Marla said you'd get brown lung disease like the coal miners and die by the time you were forty. Marla knew these things to be true because her mother graduated from nursing school and was a registered nurse.

Marla's older sister Jackie said the scariest people in the world live between the pillars under the Jeffery Boulevard viaduct. She said the mostly-bald, one-legged lady lives there, the one who sells newspapers on the corner of 79th and Jeffery, kitty-corner from the Hi-Low grocery store, just across Jeffery Boulevard from the big old Catholic church.

Nectarios agreed with Jackie and added that she very clearly was cursed by "the Evil Eye." Spyridon, Nectarios' younger brother, said he overheard Yaya, their grandmother from Crete, muttering to herself, "The bald one is cursed."

Of course, we had no idea at the time which "bald one" Yaya was referring to, but we all assumed she meant the mostly-bald, one-legged woman. We later learned, however, that Yaya's bald one was none other than Stavros Necropolis, the skin-headed grocer at Groceryland on 100th Street. Yaya once personally introduced Necropolis to her dreaded "Evil Eye" after she discovered that the pound of "imported Greek Feta" he'd sold her was actually made in Athens, *Georgia*.

You always knew something major was happening when Yaya began spitting and crossing herself all over. Just what it meant though, wasn't always clear. Yaya frequently slipped into a trance, lit tall skinny candles, and stuck them in a box of kitty litter near her Jesus artwork. Sometimes she muttered in Greek, and at other times, she sang strange Greek songs. Stevie and I relied on Nectarios and Spyridon as our interpreters. We were mesmerized by Yaya because she was so spooky. Once she sprinkled holy water all over us. Another time she rubbed some holy oil all over my sunburn and said, "Christos loves you, Jew girl."

"Your grandmother is weirding out again," Stevie Eisner observed solemnly. "No, dope," Nectarios said. "She's having one of her Jesus visions."

"I think she had a vision that the mostly-bald, one-legged lady is possessed by the demon," solemnly interpreted Spyridon, Nectarios' younger brother. It was the curse, Spyridon continued, that forced the news lady to live between the pillars of the Jeffery Avenue viaduct near our homes on the south side of Chicago.

That day, we unanimously voted the one-legged lady the "Creepiest Lady in the Neighborhood." We also unanimously agreed to take the Paxton Avenue viaduct for a while to avoid contact with her lest we become contaminated by the curse. But none of us kept our word because we were always hoping to catch a glimpse of the one-legged woman lurking between the pillars. (We never did.)

Everyone in our neighborhood believed the viaduct was a place of great mystery. Our parents repeatedly told us, "Don't ever go under the viaduct alone." So, of course, we did. But we'd run through it as fast as we could because we believed with all our hearts something life-changing could happen there. We were willing to tempt the fates.

Within the first month of getting my driver's license, I intentionally bumped into the back of a diesel-spewing Jeffery Express bus with my Dad's '64 Chevy Bel Air, right in the middle of the viaduct. My deliberate act was done on behalf of our neighbor, Bertha Eisner, my mother's closest friend in the Manor, who was dying from metastatic breast cancer.

Why did I bump the bus? Because in one of Yaya's many Technicolor visions, she reportedly shouted that Bertha's cancer was caused by fumes from the #10 Jeffery Express, the bus that connected our little neighborhood to the rest of Chicagoland. We all hated watching Bertha waste away. We blamed the stinking bus fumes because we all believed Yaya's visions predicted the evil forces at work in our neighborhood.

Exactly where was this place called the Manor, our little patch of urban paradise? We lived about six miles south of Hyde Park, three miles south of South Shore, and less than one mile south of Pill Hill (where the doctors and lawyers and their manicured wives and entitled kids lived in big single-family houses). We lived one mile north of South Deering and Trumbull Park, one mile due east of the polluted swamps, and north of the Cal-Sag Channel. We lived about two miles west of the steel mills. We lived a few miles north and east of Roseland, the Sherwin-Williams plant, the old Pullman railroad community, and home of Gately's People's Store (the building was destroyed by fire in 2019). We lived close enough to Lake Michigan to smell rotting dead alewives on the shore on a windy day, and too close to the incinerator at 103rd Street and Doty.

I wonder if an archaeologist might one day find our graffiti on those viaduct walls, after sifting through layers of soot, somewhere beneath more layers of other generations' artwork. If so, our artful creations just might be uncovered. Over the years, we documented every neighborhood romance that we knew about with hearts ("Lenny loves Debbie" and "Bruce loves Janis") and posted many phone numbers ("For a good time, call..."). Some among us drew nasty-looking pornographic creations in minute detail on the walls under the Jeffery viaduct.

A few really important events happened under the viaducts. For example, I knew—at age five—that I was going to marry Stevie Eisner. I even told him so as we were riding in the back seat of my father's car. Stevie was eight months older than me. Back in those days, Stevie and I spent many hours together, mostly enmeshed in a love-hate relationship. In the warm weather, we played ball outside with Marky and other neighbors. In the winter, we made snow igloos and snow forts and had some near-lethal snowball fights. Much of the time I adored Stevie, and I think the feelings were mutual. But the rest of the time, our loving relationship regressed drastically; he'd get mad at me and would punch me in the arm, stomach, and nose. I'd kick him in the shins. Really hard. We both cried.

My ever-optimistic mom focused on the "love" story and steadfastly refused to defend me when the gears shifted to the "hate" mode. I turned to Marla's mom to advocate for me when the bruises from Stevie became painful, noticeable, and abundant.

One night at dinnertime, when my latest Stevie-induced injuries were on full display, my father inquired about the source of my bruises. When I ratted out Stevie, my father's eyebrows went up. "Stevie's pretty strong," my father quietly noted while dousing Mother's meatloaf with a Red Sea-sized portion of Heinz ketchup. "He's also a lot bigger than you are."

My father remained uncharacteristically quiet during dinner, similar to the eerie calm we would experience in Chicago when the sky turned yellowy-pink just before a tornado would rip through the city. This comparison was not hyperbolic. It was based in truth. I noticed that the big, wormy vein on the side of my father's head was throbbing really hard. So did Mother. We knew this was not a good sign. A storm was brewing.

There was one thing almost everybody on our block knew about my father: You did not want to piss him off. As my mom and I watched the purple in his face move up his bald head, and as his neck veins visibly pulsated, we knew we wanted to be anywhere but around my father. His outbursts were well known to family, neighbors, and friends alike, especially on warm summer days when the windows were open, and you could hear my father rage all the way down the street. Apparently, everyone on our street knew about my father's temper—except Stevie.

After dinner that night, my dad casually sauntered to the curb in front of the Pincus' house where Stevie and Marky were playing a ball game called "bounce or fly." My father yanked Stevie up by his collar, dumped him headfirst into our steel garbage can, and clamped on the lid. Then he kicked the can over and continued to kick it down the street until it came to a rest in the middle of 97th Street. Neighbors up and down the block heard Stevie's screams and viewed this after-dinner entertainment with some amusement. Nobody intervened.

Margaret McDougall, our next-door neighbor, just sighed and said, "Eddie is at it again. He should learn to control that temper of his." Yeah, right.

Fortunately for my father, 1962 was still part of the halcyon times when one simply did not worry about lawsuits after teaching a lesson to a neighbor kid. My father's act—which clearly crossed the line of neighborliness—was not an entirely out-of-the-ordinary occurrence in our neighborhood. (It is probably worth noting that Stevie and I never got married to each other.)

Beyond serving as our local "art museum" and brown lung disease cluster zone, the viaduct was an important geographic wonder of Chicagoland. It was our very own version of the Continental Divide, as the viaduct clearly distinguished our piece of Chicago from the rest of the city. Generally, those living south of the viaduct from 95th Street to 103rd Street were the only ones who regularly went through it because our neighbors to the north were too scared by what they thought they'd find there.

But what those to the north never knew was that on our side of the tracks, just west of Route 41, lay paradise within the confines of a neighborhood familiarly called "The Manor." The name of our neighborhood was an unlikely choice because in the place we lived, one of America's first planned post-WWII urban communities of small, almost identical and very affordable duplex and row houses (and a few single-family homes owned by slightly more affluent land barons)—there was no similarity whatsoever to anything even remotely resembling a "manor." Actually, there were two adjacent Manors: Jeffery Manor and Merrionette Manor. Jeffery Manor wrapped around Merrionette Manor, forming one contiguous Manor. From our perspective, the neighborhood could have been named Camelot.

North of the viaduct, one found the heart and soul of Chicago: Frank Lloyd Wright's urban prairie architecture, Mies van der Rohe's famous glass curtain wall architecture, buildings of the Bauhaus design. North of the viaduct stood Chicago's best-known landmarks: Sears Tower (later named Willis Tower), the John Hancock Building, the Prudential Building, and O'Hare and Midway airports. We traveled under the viaduct to the Chicago Loop; the Museum of Science and Industry; the Field Museum; the University of Chicago; Loyola, DePaul, Roosevelt and Northwestern Universities; the Art Institute; Adler Planetarium; Shedd Aquarium; Lincoln Park and Brookfield Zoos; the Gold Coast; North Michigan Avenue; the city's best beaches; and, of course, the respective stadiums of the Bears, Bulls, Blackhawks, White Sox, and Cubs.

South of the viaduct lay one subdivision of row houses, another subdivision of duplex houses, a few Chicago-style single-family bungalows, some stores, a Little League field, Kiddieland Amusement Park, elementary schools and churches, swampland, the city garbage dump, the sewage canal, Lake Calumet, the Calumet River and its polluted tributaries, Calumet Harbor, Calumet Beach, the "East Side," and absolutely nothing of any aesthetic interest.

In fact, the area south of the viaduct might only be of real interest to toxicologists and epidemiologists studying the environmental and adverse health effects on those living on a landfill composed of hazardous waste from the steel mills and other chemical-producing factories that dumped toxic ooze on our little piece of paradise.

A comprehensive study completed by the Environmental Protection Agency in 1991 closely examined areas in Southeast Chicago and Northwest Indiana that had significant levels of air pollution, soil contamination, groundwater contamination, and wildlife toxicity. (While they didn't specifically look at the asbestos used in many houses built before 1950, that also likely added to the toxicity to which we were exposed.)

The U.S. Environmental Protection Agency (EPA) study concluded that our zip code—60617—accounted for more than 14 percent of the total volatile organic compound emissions for the entire study area of Cook County, Illinois. Unbeknown to those of us who lived under the viaduct, we were inhaling carbon dioxide, sulfur dioxide, nitrogen dioxide, chlorofluorocarbons, lead, methylene chloride, benzene, and other toxic chemicals daily. How many of us—in addition to our grandparents, parents, relatives, and neighbors—were diagnosed with asthma, autoimmune diseases, chronic obstructive pulmonary disease, emphysema, lung cancers, and other cancers as a result of our polluted air, soil, and water? Or from ingesting the poisons sprayed in the air on our streets during mosquito season?

Dichlorodiphenyltrichloroethane (DDT) was widely used as an insecticide during our childhood years. It wasn't until 1972 that it was banned because of its harmful environmental effects and the potential health risks it posed to humans. Scientists know now that these long-lasting toxins accumulated and have persisted in the environment.

Some of our Manor neighbors became very ill, often at a very young age. Some died, possibly from the effects of these and other poisons. Marla, my first friend, was diagnosed with breast cancer in her twenties. She had her first mastectomy at twenty-five. With subsequent metastases in her breastbone at twenty-nine, she survived a rare surgery at Sloan Kettering Cancer Center in New York that excised her sternum, breast tissue, muscle, lymph nodes, and cancer cells, and replaced them with a mesh substance and skin grafts. Thirteen years later the cancer recurred, and she had a mastectomy on her other breast. Marla lived through months of exhausting surgeries, chemotherapy and radiation oncology, repeated diagnostic imaging, and chronic angst. She is still closely monitored by her medical oncologist and by her gastroenterologist for the Crohn's disease she later developed.

Her sister, Jackie, was diagnosed with ovarian cancer in her early forties and died from metastatic disease at age forty-four.

Our neighbor, Bertha Eisner, a native of East Chicago, Indiana, and a transplant to the Manor, lived her entire life near oil refineries, polluted air and waterways, and steel mills. She died from breast cancer in her mid-forties. At least three other women on our block were diagnosed with breast cancer; two of the three died several years ago. My Aunt Essie, also a Manor resident, died from metastatic colon cancer. And these are just the people I can readily recall. There were others.

There is now sufficient evidence that our air, surface water, soil, and groundwater were all contaminated during the years my family and I lived there. The good news for newer residents of the Manor is that the levels of toxicity have diminished, due mainly to environmental regulations implemented after all the people we knew had left the area. Unhealthy levels of manganese later appeared to be of concern, according to this EPA report.

How was our little family affected? Ever since I was eight years old, I have experienced life-threatening allergic reactions and have battled both unknown and little understood invaders to my immune system from a panoply of medications, foods, food preservatives, viruses, and bacteria. Manifesting in the form of inflammatory hives at their best (and severe anaphylactic reactions at their worst), I have been rendered half-dead many times throughout my life, kept alive by steroids, epinephrine injections, asthma inhalers, Benadryl, and the loving care of my mother and, later, my husband.

What caused these chronic and acute medical conditions that have afflicted no one else I know? My parents and I learned along the way that I was severely allergic to papaya that I tasted once in Florida and that almost killed me an hour later. We also learned that papaya is an ingredient in my favorite childhood drink, Hawaiian Punch. We later discovered that Adolph's Meat Tenderizer used to contain papain, the papaya enzyme, to break down tougher meat and, unbeknown to us, ME!

And Chinese food, our favorite cuisine, was loaded with MSG, as was soy sauce and many other Asian sauces. For many years there was nothing documented in medical literature about extreme allergic reactions to papaya and MSG. We eventually learned that these substances were part of a larger group of foods and drugs known as "salicylates" that were also making me ill. The most well-known salicylate is aspirin. There are hundreds of other foods and drugs in this family.

What causes my body to have severe allergic reactions? Did environmental toxins absorbed during my childhood somehow cause a shift in my immune system that, at seemingly random times, sends me into a tailspin? I wonder today if the toxins plaguing the Manor and other nearby communities played a contributing role.

Despite living in the epidemiological wasteland south of the viaduct, former residents of the Manor still agree it was a great place to grow up—except when the huge incinerator on 103rd and Doty would belch stinking air in our direction. On those days, we called the Manor "the Manure." Nonetheless, our parents were proud to live in the Manor, deep in the environmental sewer that we called home.

It is important to note that the Manor was not simply a random assortment of tiny houses built on cheap landfill. It was a "planned community," intended to serve primarily the needs of white people of similar ages and socioeconomic backgrounds. The target population was comprised of veterans of WWII and the Korean War. The Manor was created to serve as a collective space with centralized schools, accessible and affordable shopping, and a variety of places of worship, all supported by an excellent transit system. While we were technically residents of Chicago, the Manor felt suburban because of its winding streets and its relative quiet in contrast to the rest of the city.

The Manor undoubtedly was influenced by the sociological concept of *gemeinschaft*, coined by German sociologist Ferdinand Tönnies, and in contrast to *gesellschaft*. According to Wikipedia, *gemeinschaft* emphasizes common mores and shared values in which community residents behave with a responsibility toward one another for the greater good of the community. The ultimate *gemeinschaft* community would be an Israeli kibbutz, a commune, or a cooperative, where social and economic interdependencies are planned and sustained.

By contrast, *gesellschaft* deemphasizes familial and personal relationships. In *gesellschaft* communities, individual status is obtained by personal achievement, education, and productivity. Group interdependencies are not even a consideration. Examples of this would include living in urban high-rise buildings as well as in areas where there is considerable space between dwellings.

Even fifty years after we left the Manor, many of my friends and I still yearn for its closeness, its sense of community. We reminisce and relive our glory days through our Facebook virtual communities. We now have more than 1,600 former Manor residents on one such site. What we miss most is the *gemeinschaft* we experienced—the communal spirit that was intentionally and mindfully crafted by the Manor's planners. Sadly, many who left the Manor found themselves catapulted into anonymous *gesellschaft* neighborhoods, largely as a result of growing older and moving away from family-oriented places. Consequently, very few of us have come close to replicating the communal spirit that we enjoyed as residents of the Manor.

Marla's dad and my dad enjoyed igniting various explosives for our July 4th celebrations. These included bottle rockets, railroad flares, M-80s, and other "non-nuclear" incendiary devices they'd purchased just over the state line in Indiana. As a group, we'd head over to Trumbull Park for evening fireworks or pull our lawn chairs to the grounds of the Catholic parish a half block away to view them. This was part of our communal experience, the *gemeinschaft* that still fills our collective memories.

Our parents were friendly and we Brennan Avenue kids played with other neighbor children close in age to us. When we were home in the summertime, our doors were left open and unlocked. Adults and kids went in and out of their neighbors' homes, dropping by for a friendly visit, a cup of sugar, a glass of Kool-Aid, a Band-Aid, or a chance to share a little gossip. This was life on Brennan Avenue—casual and welcoming.

Seeking perhaps to approximate our Manor experiences, some of us later moved to other "planned communities." For example, in our current community in Gilbert, Arizona, I can join the Community

Women's Club. We can sit on the homeowners' association board; join neighborhood book clubs, lunch groups, and walking groups; and participate in such community-sponsored events as the annual Easter Egg Hunt and an annual visit from Santa at the neighborhood park. We can also participate in the semiannual neighborhood garage sale and free document shredding events. Here we enjoy evening springtime concerts in our neighborhood park, and an annual holiday boat parade on our community's three lakes. In these planned neighborhoods, much like in the Manor, we are able to walk to local coffee shops and individually owned restaurants as well as other small strip mall stores.

At the same time, however, it isn't the same as it was in the Manor. We're no longer children. Our front doors are locked, and we rely on our security systems and Ring doorbells to screen unwanted visitors. The Manor clearly was conceived to be the type of community where social bonds were achieved through our neighborly relationships. But *gemeinschaft* is an idealized social concept. In truth, the social relationships in the Manor were anything but ideal.

CHAPTER TWO

North and South of the Viaducts

Compare yourself only with yourself. You don't know others' full story, and there's no need to feel guilty for not being as good as them, or feeling justified in being "better" or "worse" in any area. We all walk our own path, and we all have our own lessons and challenges to face. The more you focus on you, the better you will become.

– Doe Zantamata

Where but in the Manor would you find such memorable and diverse neighbors as Sherman Skolnick, Richard Speck, Michelle Obama, Mandy Patinkin, Steve Allen, and Mel Tormé? Well, some of them weren't exactly our neighbors, but on the south side of Chicago, they lived close enough for us to claim them as such. So, what's a few miles here or there?

My mother was reared in South Shore and graduated with Steve Allen from Hyde Park High School. Mel Tormé was a couple of years behind them. I was born in Hyde Park, moved as an infant to South Shore, and relocated as a toddler to the Manor, all mere miles apart. These South Side neighborhoods seemed, in some ways, to be extensions of the Manor because they were contiguous areas that we often frequented. Only the viaducts separated us.

We went to movie theaters and enjoyed ice cream sundaes in South Shore, just down the street from the shoe store where my parents bought my corrective saddle shoes with steel inserts. We ate hot beef and gravy sandwiches on white bread with mashed potatoes at Peter Pan in South Shore, and enjoyed eating the burgers and throwing peanut shells on the floor at Chances R in Hyde Park. Their main distinction was that they were located north of the viaduct.

When you grew up in the Manor, you claimed that everybody famous was your neighbor—or the story simply wasn't worth telling. And every South Sider I knew spoke the language of neighborliness; that is, we often made up stories about our neighbors (and swore to God they were true). Some of our tales were edgy enough to draw blood. Two talents reigned supreme on our block: telling the best story and telling the filthiest joke (my father claimed the prize for the latter). There were more virtuous talents, to be sure, but there were none nearly as memorable on our block.

Marla's dad, Natty Lerner, was king of the Manor storytellers. Natty could spin tales for hours at a time. He held his audience in rapt attention. Natty's elaborate stories always had pitch-perfect punchlines. His timing was flawless, his delivery, spot-on. Natty's laughter was like that of a hyena and his entire six-foot frame jiggled in a giant spasm as he laughed at his own stories right along with us. His cackles could be heard as far away as the Kirschbaum's on the corner of 98th Street. Natty and another neighbor, Stuie Harkness, could even talk backwards for hours on end without stopping to swallow their saliva. Natty was the best storyteller the Manor ever claimed. He was also one of the kindest people who ever lived, period. I never would have learned to drive a car if not for Natty Lerner. He was patient, good-natured, funny, and he never swore at me or the other drivers.

Marla and I inherited certain talents from our fathers, particularly the ability to create embellished—but believable—stories about our neighbors, which naturally we swore to God were true.

We told stories about one neighbor, Betty May, who walked around in her husband's socks and sandals, and favored faded muumuus. She chain-smoked Tiparillos. She was a strange woman, the mother of two strange young children. Her husband was a quiet fellow who kept to himself and avoided social interactions. This family became low-hanging fruit, ripe for picking for our fertile little imaginations.

Marla told me many years later that Betty May and her husband became wealthy and maintained a high profile in Chicago's Jewish philanthropic organizations after they moved to the North Shore. Marla said she was shocked to learn that Betty May traded in her muumuus and her husband's footwear in favor of ball gowns and heels, as seen in society photos in the Chicago's *Jewish Press*. It's a stretch for me to imagine Betty May sporting Jimmy Choos instead of her husband's leather sandals.

They lived near the Levy family. My mother said that Lavergne Levy answered her phone speaking French. She refused to switch to English, at least when my mother called. It is worth noting that Lavergne was one hundred percent American with English as her primary language and Yiddish as her second. Unfortunately, my mom did not speak French (and only remembered a little high school Spanish). Fortunately, my mom knew just enough French to say "au revoir" to Lavergne. Her husband, Myron, who sported a jaunty little French beret, was just a tad bit "off."

Another one of our favorite targets was a neighbor up the street, a forlorn and frumpy single woman who lived with her brother. In our own friendly South Side way, Marky, Stevie, and I pelted her with crabapples outside her brother's house. She avoided her front yard after a particularly good yield from the crabapple tree.

Clearly, we were not the most sensitive children.

The way I coped best with our weird neighbors and crazy family members was by forming strong attachments to my beloved pets. When I was a toddler, my father acquired a duck that followed me around our backyard. Later, he gave his pet duck to a friend who cooked it for Sunday dinner. Apparently, my father hadn't formed a healthy attachment to "Donald."

I've had dogs in my life from the time I was four, starting with a black cocker spaniel named Lady. After Lady's death from congestive heart failure, my parents thought that a parakeet would be a good substitute for a dog. We had several parakeets over a few years. The most memorable was our last.

My father decided—for no good reason—that the parakeet's toenails needed to be trimmed. Apparently an aspiring pet podiatrist, he wielded his mighty clippers and did a number on our pet bird. I had never before seen a bird rotate 180 degrees on its perch. After suffering for a short time after that, the poor parakeet mercifully ascended to its heavenly perch.

We also had our share of goldfish in small fishbowls, generally obtained from carnivals at our temple. The goldfish were prizes if you were lucky enough to throw a ping-pong ball and have it land in one of their bowls. I was lucky on numerous occasions, but unhappy to learn that each of my goldfish was suicidal. After a day in our house— probably in fear of my father—we found each goldfish plastered to the linoleum floor in our basement, jumping from their captivity, unwilling to face their earthly fates in our home.

When I was eight, my father decided that he just had to own a baby alligator and purchased one for $3 at a souvenir store on Collins Avenue in Miami Beach. It came in a sturdy cardboard carrier outfitted with air holes that he transported to Chicago in February of 1960. The alligator was cute until it started growing rapidly. As most alligators do, it tried to bite our fingers off each time we fed it. My father's pet alligator quickly outgrew the basement sink and died after a few months. We buried the alligator in our backyard. I wonder what archaeologists will one day conclude when the alligator's remains are excavated from our former backyard on Chicago's South Side.

After that, we returned to dogs and acquired Tammy from the Animal Welfare Society shelter when I was in sixth grade. Tammy was an adorable cocker spaniel/yellow lab mix, and she filled our home with her abundant sweetness.

Marla had beautiful collies, starting with Princess. Her older sister had a pet monkey that became a major attraction for the children on our block. Other neighbors owned shelties, a beagle, and a toy poodle. One neighbor "owned" feral cats, one of which gave me a deep scratch on my neck, leading to a long-time aversion to cats.

In addition to our weird neighbors, crazy family members, and eclectic assortment of pets, we actually had a few normal human friends living on our block. Our good friend Marky lived in the duplex just north of Marla. Marky and Stevie were best friends and were inseparable. Marky's dad died when he was very young and left his young widow to raise their two sons. Marky's ancient Eastern European grandma—known to all as "Bubby"—lived with them, mainly to keep an eye on Marky and his older brother when their mom was running the family business. Natty Lerner took on the role of surrogate dad to Marky and taught him almost everything he needed to know to become a man.

A defining memory etched forever in my mind was the sight and sound of Bubby out in front of Marky's house calling his name in her thick Eastern European accent, especially late on Friday afternoons in anticipation of Shabbat dinner. The heavenly fragrance of Bubby's homemade challah bread wafted down the street, reminding us all that Friday was a very special day indeed.

Marky and I created a "Swear Jar" in which we collected dimes every time we caught one another or our neighbors and relatives swearing. Our goal was to save up enough change to buy comic books. We probably could have bought a Mercedes with all the dimes we collected. We gained immunity, however, when we sat in our "Swear Tent," constructed of sofa cushions and my dad's Army blanket. In our tent—large enough to fully ensconce Marky, Stevie, and me—we cursed to our collective hearts' content with no penalties imposed.

We also spent hours playing with little green plastic soldiers in Marky's basement, shooting cat's eye marbles, attempting round-the-worlds with our Duncan yo-yos, hitting paddle balls, and playing Monkey in the Middle with 16-inch softballs and Stevie. Every now and then, other duplex neighbor kids joined in on the fun.

Southsiders had their own common language, especially the Jewish folks who lived there. For example, the official South Side Jewish code for another Jew was "M.O.T.," meaning "Member of the Tribe." Marla claimed the term was translated from ancient Aramaic scrolls found in caves near the Dead Sea. Stevie said she was right and added that he learned this important fact from Rabbi Rashnikoff at Hebrew School. I also learned this codified language at an early age from my parents. We vacationed one year in Washington, D.C., and waited in a long line to get into the White House. Suddenly, my mother saw some people in line, and she whispered loudly to my father, "Look, Eddie, there are M.O.T.s." I was glad I knew the ancient code so I could understand what she was saying. What comfort my mother derived in knowing that, even in our nation's capital, we were not alone.

Non-Jews were "goyim" in the plural or "goy" in the singular, a term used in such commonly uttered sentences as, "Don't date goyim because their parents worked in concentration camps and ate Jewish children for breakfast." I heard that one a lot, especially in reference to Nectarios and Spyridon.

Nectarios and Spyridon were first-generation Greek-American brothers who lived in a really creepy bungalow near 100th Street. Their home smelled like spinach, lamb, and incense. This combination of odors was so thick that I tried to breathe through my mouth whenever I was in their house. My thick hair always smelled like lamb and incense after a visit.

Strange-colored pictures with winged angels, and Jesus and Mary with gold plates behind their heads were hung on just about every wall of their home. "Icons," Spyridon called them, but Stevie and Marla called them "Ickies." Yaya, who always looked like she needed a good shave, crept along the walls while kissing pictures of these angel people. We elected Yaya Pappas, who always seemed to be enshrouded in black, to be "Second Creepiest Lady of the Neighborhood" on a day when the brothers weren't around. We suspected that Yaya lived under the viaduct, too, although Nectarios insisted she lived in their attic.

Among our most celebrated neighbors, only Sherman Skolnick, a Polio-stricken, eccentric, conspiracy-theorist writer, and mass murderer Richard Speck actually lived in—or hung out in—the Manor. Speck became the highest profile drifter in our neighborhood after he murdered eight student nurses in the summer of 1966, just across 100th Street from our elementary school. In fact, more than fifty years later, I still ask people if they remember Richard Speck. When they say, "Yeah, he's the guy who killed all those nurses," I tell them he was my neighbor, in order to establish exactly where I grew up. Speck's notoriety has inspired such memorable dialogue as:

"You really grew up in Speck's neighborhood? Did you know him?"

"Of course. He signed my autograph book in eighth grade."

"Was he spooky?"

"Only when he wasn't drunk."

"Did he ever expose himself?"

"Yeah. You shoulda seen the size of his tattoo."

My mother and I were out on the night of July 13, 1966, with my friend Wilma and her mom Adele, wheeling around in Adele's little black Volvo. Adele smoked cigarettes and discovered that she needed another pack. Before dropping us off at home late that night, we stopped at the Clark Gas Station on 100th Street to pick up her cigarettes. The gas station was kitty-corner from the student nurses' townhouse. We were there at precisely the time Speck was torturing, raping, and murdering his prey. Fortunately, one of the student nurses hid under a bunk bed undiscovered and survived to tell the story. She identified Speck when she saw the "Born to Raise Hell" tattoo on his arm after he was found on Chicago's Skid Row.

The next morning, our phone rang at 6 a.m. My Uncle Jacob, an attorney, called to inform us of the mass murder. He told my dad that one of his clients was the father of one of the victims. He invited my dad to accompany him to the murder scene. By the time they arrived, the townhouse was already cordoned off, the police and media were present, and curious neighbors milled around the area.

In the small world in which we lived, sixteen years after this brutal killing, I worked with the brother of one of Speck's victims, a medical oncologist at a Catholic hospital in Urbana, Illinois, where he was the medical director of our new hospice program. Many years later, after he found a box of old photos and slides in his basement in Mahomet, Illinois, he was interviewed by the *Chicago Tribune* about his sister Nina. (A book, *Nina's Smile*, was written and published by Terry Cremin, a former Manorite, about this doctor's late sister.)

After the Speck murders, we swore to God (with our fingers and toes crossed) that we saw Speck over at the Tastee Freez on 100th Street, about 100 feet from where he became Chicago's most well-known mass murderer (this was before John Wayne Gacy), just across from Benny the Kosher Butcher's and the Maritime Union Hall. We mostly said we knew Richard Speck to drive our parents crazy. Truth is, we were scared to go over to 100th Street after that. Some of my friends stopped collecting pop bottles for change at the Clark Gas Station that summer, stopped shopping at Groceryland and Sol's Drug Store, and pretty much declared 100th Street to be no man's land. The only reason left to go there was to catch the Jeffery Express bus to go downtown. Or to point to the tiny little townhouse shrine to show visitors where eight student nurses died, tragically and far too young. Benny's closed down a few years after Richard Speck's night of terror. There was very little demand for his penny candy and skinny little kosher chickens after that.

Mandy Patinkin lived just a few miles away, north of the viaduct that separated our shoebox subdivision of duplexes from the "important" people who could afford single-family houses. Actually, Mandy didn't regard us as his neighbors and he probably didn't know any of us at all. But when we watched him sing his preteen heart out in performances at the Jewish Youth Center in South Shore, he became our collective heartthrob. (Mothers decreed him as "such a talented boychik" and he was elected our "cutest neighbor.")

And then there were Steve Allen and Mel Tormé, a generation removed, but we claimed them as our neighbors, too.

Michelle Robinson Obama, considerably younger than we were, lived a few miles north of the viaduct. Her family home was a block away from my pediatrician's office and my mother's podiatrist. In her book, *Becoming*, Ms. Obama's affinity for her South Side neighborhood of origin was strong, enduring, and fully relatable. She, too, experienced the community spirit of the South Side, although as a child of color growing up there, her perspective was very different from my own. As whites fled the area, her neighborhood transitioned from an integrated middle-class neighborhood to a Black neighborhood and later still to a troubled Black community with high rates of crime.

In the Manor, we also had our local neighborhood heroes. Brothers Gus and Alex Pappas, owners of Pappas Bros. Mt. Athos Cleaners Extraordinaire ("For Memerible Baptisms, Proms and Weddings"), were local heroes among the Manor's Jews because of their "half-off speshals." Nectarios, Gus' oldest son, delivered my dad's shirts on Fridays. Nectarios was the object of my first major crush when I was in the seventh grade. One year, on the first night of Chanukah, Nectarios dropped off some shirts and my dad asked him if he was circumcised. Dad even offered to do the job for him if he wasn't. Nectarios swore he'd never set foot in our house again! My dad told me that the look on Nectarios' face was a fitting Chanukah gift because it symbolized "the fall of the Greek empire."

Nectarios Pappas and Dinky Kekich were best friends, and they were our friends too. Although they weren't M.O.T.s, I thought they were great guys. Along with Marla, Marky, and Stevie, they were my closest friends in the Manor.

We white Jewish kids from the Manor weren't rich, but we enjoyed aspects of white privilege that we were not even aware of. Our homes were tiny, but we had roofs over our heads, food on the table, and clothing to wear. And we had nonstop access to television.

Television occupied a huge part of our young lives in the Manor. Most of us didn't enjoy color TV until the late 1960s, so our viewing was done on those big, boxy black-and-white sets. Marla's TV was shaped like a gas pump. I also remember visiting the Eisners' grand-parents' home in East Chicago, Indiana, and seeing their brand-new color TV, long before any of us had one. We gathered around that TV as if we were venerating an icon.

On Saturday mornings, Mom and I watched Dick Clark and American Bandstand. I loved watching Lassie, Fury, Bugs Bunny, and other cartoons, among scores of other children's shows.

When we were a little older, we enjoyed the Beatles' American debut on *The Ed Sullivan Show*. Still later, we watched *Bonanza*,

Gunsmoke, Laugh-In, Hullabaloo, and *The Smothers Brothers.* We were definitely children of the media, mesmerized by the sights and sounds transmitted into our homes each day. Most of the shows we viewed were pure entertainment. Others were more serious.

After leaving school at noon on November 22, 1963 to go home for lunch, I overheard one of the patrol boys (also known as crossing guards) on 99th Street say that President Kennedy had been shot. I remember responding, "That's such a mean thing to say!"

When I entered our house a few minutes later, I saw my mom glued to the television set, tears streaming down her face. She was watching Walter Cronkite on CBS. We ate lunch together on TV trays in front of the television. Shortly before I returned to my sixth-grade classroom, we saw Cronkite fight back tears as he delivered the news that JFK had been shot in the head in Dallas and had just been confirmed dead at Parkland Hospital. We spent the rest of the afternoon at school watching news footage on our classroom televisions along with our weeping teachers.

Also, that day, we watched JFK's bloodstained young widow witness the transfer of presidential power to Lyndon B. Johnson. And a few days after that, we as a nation collectively gathered to observe the television broadcast of JFK's funeral procession and viewed close-up reactions of Jackie Kennedy and the grief-stricken family. Little John-John's salute to his father's flag-draped coffin became an iconic TV image.

Television brought other powerful images, including that of Jack Ruby fatally shooting Lee Harvey Oswald, the alleged murderer of John F. Kennedy, two days after the president's assassination. And another at the Lorraine Motel in Memphis, where Martin Luther King, Jr., was assassinated on April 4, 1968. Two months later, television cameramen recorded vivid images of a dying Bobby Kennedy lying on the floor of a Los Angeles hotel kitchen with his eyes wide open, shortly after he'd won the California presidential primary. And the iconic images of war protests at Kent State University on May 4, 1970, that tragically ended with the fatal shootings of four unarmed students by members of the Ohio National Guard.

As a generation, we grew immune to gory footage of the bloodshed in Vietnam's jungles transmitted nightly to our TV screens. But two vivid images stand out to this day: that of a young, horrified Vietnamese girl running naked after a napalm attack, and the other of a traumatized Vietnamese man being shot in the head.

For better or worse, we were children of the media.

Chapter Three

The Sociological Intersection
North, South, and East of the Viaducts

On July 20, 1969, a group of teens gathered at my cousin Jenny's Manor duplex to watch Apollo 11 Astronauts Neil Armstrong and Buzz Aldrin take those first tentative steps on the lunar surface 239,000 miles from Earth. Among the group of us who witnessed this historic event were the boys Jenny and I married a few years later. If my memory serves me correctly, this might have been the final gathering of this group of friends before the great white Manor exodus.

Almost entirely white until 1967, the Manor was a "mixed" neighborhood of blue- and white-collar workers, war vets with high school diplomas who were just getting started in their careers at shoe stores, auto yards, and retail stores. Hardworking folks, they stayed busy eking out a living and creating families with their post-war brides producing a generation of upwardly mobile baby boomers: us.

Among the elder folk, there was a smattering of college-educated people, including our maternal grandfather, a dentist who practiced in South Shore and lived in the Manor with our grandmother, whom we affectionately called Nonny. A Russian Jew born in 1885, our grandfather (we called him Papa and Baldy) and his family immigrated to Chicago's Maxwell Street Jewish ghetto around 1900. With his fair skin and red hair, he looked more Irish than Jewish. That, along with his non-ethnic-sounding surname that had been Anglicized on Ellis Island, helped him gain entry to Loyola Dental School, a Jesuit university from which he proudly graduated. Papa established his dental practice at 67th and Stony Island in South Shore and drove to the Manor after living in apartments in South Shore for many years. In the Manor, he grew his beloved rhubarb plants alongside their spacious garage. Marla and I played in their backyard so she could flirt with the boy who lived behind them on Yates.

In the late 1930s, my grandparents and some of their Jewish immigrant dentist friends built summer cabins in Michiana Shores, a Lake Michigan beach town on the Indiana/Michigan border east of Chicago, just beyond Michigan City, Indiana.

On Friday afternoons in the summer, my grandpa and his friends rode the orange South Shore Line commuter train from Chicago to the Michigan City depot. From there, they often caught the bus that slowly wound its way along numerous bus stops up the shore to Michiana. One such stop was Beverly Shores, an exclusive village that boldly displayed signs proclaiming, "No Jews allowed." (My grandparents said Jews frequently experienced this type of discrimination. Even the South Shore Country Club on 71st Street was known to be anti-Semitic.)

My grandma, mother, and aunt spent entire summers at the Michiana cabin, away from Chicago. Sadly, they sold the cabin shortly before I was born. Nonetheless, we returned to the area many times over the years to go to the beach and to drive by their beloved summer home.

Michiana Shores holds an important place in my family's history. My Aunt Essie met her future husband, Jacob, on the Michiana beach. Later, my mom met her future husband—my dad—on the same beach. Turns out, the beach at the bus's Stop 38 was the "spawning ground" where numerous WWII Jewish veterans and their soon-to-be brides, some ultimately on their way to pursuing lives in the Manor, first met.

Before the Chicago Skyway and Indiana Toll Road were built, we made the sixty-five mile drive to Michiana from the Manor on Routes 12–20 into and beyond Whiting, Hammond, and Gary, Indiana, the area known for its putrid oil refineries that turned the sky an opaque yellow. We rolled up our car windows when driving past Wolf Lake, past the Illinois/Indiana border into Whiting, East Chicago, and east of Gary, Indiana. The stinking air burned our eyes and throats. Once away from the refineries, the air became breathable and the landscape gradually transitioned to sand dunes and bucolic countryside. We were finally free of the toxins that literally plagued us.

Our frequent summer trips to Michiana included stops at the Michigan City beach and zoo, and on Franklin Street, the main drag, a visit to Scholl's Dairy (with the big white milk bottle on its roof) for a hot fudge ice cream sundae. Later, we'd stop at Hickory Pit for delicious fried chicken with biscuits and honey. Our family picnics on beach blankets, complete with roving bands of ants, were always both a challenge and a delight.

Near the end of my mother's life, on a trip back to Chicago, she and I enjoyed a spontaneous drive to Michiana after a visit to White Castle for a blast from the past. We wanted to drive by the beloved cabin and see other familiar sites. I think we both knew we'd never make this trip together again.

On a whim, we stopped by the old cabin and knocked on the door. A young woman answered. My mom, then eighty years old, told her, "We are visiting from Arizona. My parents built this cabin when I was a teenager, many years ago." Much to our delight, the current occupant enthusiastically greeted us and invited us into the cabin. She told us that she and her brother, who was a real estate developer in the area, inherited the cabin from their grandparents from Cicero. She said only one other family had owned the cabin after my grandparents sold it.

"Please tell me what is original and what was added on later," she implored. My mother responded, showing her the original "sleeping porch" used by my aunt and my mom and their friends who visited from Chicago on summer weekends.

Later, my mom and I were gifted with photographs of the beloved cabin taken by this delightful young woman, as well as a couple of photos of the two of us that she snapped in front of the home. We agreed that Nonny and Papa would have been very pleased with our visit. We couldn't have been happier! On our way home, memories of Nonny and Papa danced through our heads, sparking wonderful stories.

Nonny was an independent, intelligent, highly opinionated woman. When she wasn't in Michiana, she assisted Papa in his dental practice or babysat me at their Manor home while my mom worked with my dad at their short-lived "variety store" in Mount Greenwood.

In the Manor, Nonny prepared my favorite lunches: fried smelts or sardines on white bread, spread with onions and schmaltz (rendered chicken fat). I also loved sandwiches made with extra-sharp cheddar that my cousin Jenny and I called "smelly cheese." Black Cows (a glass of Pepsi and a scoop of vanilla ice cream) were lovingly prepared for us by Nonny. And nobody's sugar cookies could ever compare.

Papa retired from his dental practice in 1959 after receiving a blunt force blow to his head, from what we don't know. He was found unconscious and required hospitalization and rehabilitation. Eventually, the harsh Chicago winters became unbearable for them and so they decided to move to Miami Beach. We visited them there every February and stayed at a faded art deco hotel near the beach, several blocks from their one-bedroom apartment. My grandfather spent much of his time learning Spanish, later teaching Spanish at a nearby senior center. (Note: He reportedly spoke eight different languages!)

After a few years, they bought a larger condominium in North Miami Beach where they spent much of their time taking long walks around the grounds, clipping coupons to use at Publix, and working on lovely mosaic plates and tables, a few of which we still own and display in our home.

On one family outing in 1962, we visited a shopping mall in North Miami Beach where I noticed something I'd never seen before: restroom signs for "colored men" and "colored women" and a water fountain designated for "coloreds." I asked my mother why they had these signs up. She shushed me and whispered, "We'll talk about it when we get back to Nonny and Papa's."

Her explanation about segregation in the southern states was mind-blowing for this ten-year-old girl. I grew up in the north in a very diverse population and without separate racially designated comfort stations. What we saw in Florida just didn't seem fair or right. It wasn't.

Back in the Manor in the middle of February, with our Florida tans and our cheap souvenirs, life went on at the usual pace. While many Manor residents were tradesmen, shop owners, salespeople, and undereducated regular Joes, occasionally one would find a pedigreed neighbor or family member. On our block, we had an actual PhD living across the street. Marla's duplex neighbor was a professor of English literature at Indiana University's East Chicago campus. Before he and his family moved in, a psychiatrist and his family lived in that duplex but later migrated to a swanky North Shore suburb.

The Manor boasted a smattering of other intelligentsia, including a college professor who wrote the chemistry workbook we used at our high school. Our Irish Catholic next-door neighbor, father of six daughters and one son, had a bachelor's degree and taught school. My mother was just one semester shy of earning her bachelor's degree in education at DePaul University. She left school after three and a half years due to a severe bout of pneumonia. She never completed her degree. Essie, her older sister, earned a bachelor's degree at Indiana University, and later a master's degree, and was married to an attorney.

The more well-educated, wealthier, professional white folks mainly lived in neighborhoods north of the viaduct in single-family homes. Most of these "northerners" weren't even aware of their poorer brethren south of the viaduct until they heard the news about the infamous Richard Speck and how he murdered so many student nurses.

We of the Manor were assigned to the high school north of the viaduct long before—and after—Blacks moved into our neighborhoods. Blockbusting, profit-driven realtors began whipping our neighbors into a frenzy. As a result, most of the Jews living on the South Side began a modern white exodus in the late 1960s and early 1970s. Most white families on both sides of the viaduct had left the area by 1972 as part of this well-choreographed "white flight." White suburbs were the new "promised land" with the promise of better schools, nicer neighborhoods, and a lack of racial diversity.

Our white exodus from the South Side coincided with the Great Northward Migration of Blacks from southern states where they had experienced bitter racial discrimination for more than 100 years after the Civil War. What catalyzed this migration that occurred roughly between 1915 and 1975 were a series of untenable new laws passed in the South that created poll taxes, literacy tests, and other measures to keep citizens of color under the thumbs of powerful white officials and employers. Strict segregation through Jim Crow laws was enforced throughout the Southern United States. (Note: By 1838, the term "Jim Crow" was used as a collective racial slur for southern Blacks.) Pushback from Blacks, many of whom were barely able to survive, led to violence from white supremacist groups, including the Ku Klux Klan. Lynching of Blacks who rebelled against this white authority occurred in the South in the 1960s and continued into the 1980s.

The Great Northward Migration spurred an estimated six million African Americans to move from rural southern towns to those farther north and west. By 1970, more than eighty percent of African Americans nationwide lived in northern cities in Black-dominated neighborhoods, including Chicago. For many Blacks that moved northward, the living conditions were often not much better than what they experienced in the South. Housing and lending restrictions and racial discrimination in the North continued to be a very real part of their Black experience.

The white exodus from Chicago's South Side started just a few short years after passage of The Civil Rights Act of 1964, which ended segregation in public places and banned employment discrimination on the basis of race, color, religion, sex, or national origin. Congress later expanded the act and passed additional civil rights legislation, including the Voting Rights Act of 1965.

It blows my mind when I realize that I was already thirteen years old when Black women were first given the right to vote in our country (Asian American women were given this right in 1952, the year I was born, and Native American women in 1957), and that I was fifteen years old when Martin Luther King, Jr., was assassinated, and when "white flight" started in earnest on both sides of the viaduct.

As noted by author Robin DiAngelo:

> "...we are taught that we lose nothing of value through racial segregation. Consider the message we send to our children—as well as to children of color—when we describe white segregation as good."

The exodus of whites from newly integrated South Side neighborhoods during The Great Migration of Blacks northward is historically significant. Add to that the recent end of WWII and the subsequent emancipation of thousands of European Jews and other minorities from Nazi death camps, and the effect is an incredible thirty-year period of racial and ethnic discrimination and social transformation, all of which affected Chicago's South Side neighborhoods.

Chapter Four

Life in the Manor Before White Flight

Before the white exodus, the Manor was an idyllic place of religious diversity. Many of the Jews in the Manor attended either Congregation Beth Israel (CBI), the local conservative synagogue, or another conservative temple just north of the viaduct. Other non-conservative Jews were affiliated with reform or ethnic-oriented temples in South Shore and Hyde Park. At the time I lived in the Manor, there was one Orthodox Jewish synagogue in South Chicago.

We had a large Roman Catholic parish and Catholic school at the southern end of our block, just across 99th Street from our public school and due south of the Dog Doo Trail (where dogs could do their "thing"). Across the street and due east of our school were a small Baptist Church and the neighborhood synagogue. To the south, just north of 100th Street, was a large nondenominational community church, home to my Girl Scout troop. And to the west of our public school was a small Lutheran church. The smattering of Greeks in the Manor attended the big Greek Orthodox Church on Stony Island in South Shore, and the few Serbs in our neighborhood went to the Serbian Orthodox Church at 98th and Commercial. Though mostly Jewish and Catholic, the Manor was decidedly religiously inclusive. During my childhood, the neighborhood was lily-white and was actually planned to be that way, as we learned later.

Many public-school kids in the Manor cut through the Catholic School property to have a shorter walk to the elementary school. This was especially helpful in the snowy winter months, as we regularly went home for lunch at noon and then had to be back to school by 1 p.m.

Knowing this, Father McAfee somehow trained his German Shepherd to sniff out non-Catholic flesh. At least that was the rumor many of us subscribed to. I believe it, because I was viciously attacked by the priest's dog on my way home from the bus stop during my sophomore year of high school. Father McAfee witnessed (and I'm convinced, encouraged) the attack from a distance on the church property. Fortunately, my thick winter coat and mohair sweater were a protective buffer against the dog's teeth. I escaped with a ripped coat sleeve, a sore arm—and acute traumatic stress—and was relieved when his dog eventually spotted a bird that he was more interested in eating than me.

It was widely known that Father McAfee and his associates, Father Johnny Salvaggio and Father Nino Pomodoro, looked unkindly on non-Catholics walking across church property, even during intensely cold weather even when the shortcut shaved at least ten minutes off our walks in the frozen tundra.

The parochial school kids and the public-school kids generally ignored each other while en route to our respective schools, even when we cut across their property to get to our school. What happened after school hours was a different matter entirely. One former Manorite, Paul Mazursky—an unusually large Jewish kid—recalled getting bullied and beaten up by some Catholic schoolboys. Forty years later, he was still so incensed by the memory of these experiences that he didn't want to associate with any of his former Catholic neighbors, not even on a nostalgic Manor Facebook page. Interestingly if not ironically, before his tragic death, Paul shared a happy life with his second wife, a lovely Catholic woman.

Did the priest intentionally "sic" his dog on me because I wasn't a member of his parish? Did Paul experience blatant anti-Semitism?

Were some Jewish kids guilty of taunting their gentile neighbors and vice versa? The answers to these questions were probably "yes."

Importantly though, what we all shared in the Manor far outweighed our differences. Our little duplex houses had the architectural detail of a Post Toasties box, with the most notable distinction being that the actual cereal box was probably larger and more well-insulated. Our slightly more affluent neighbors two doors down had a detached garage. They built a vestibule for wet boots and a dormer on their attic to add bedroom space and a second bathroom. They even added a plywood vanity cabinet to hide the pipe under the bathroom sink! We all went over to see the vanity the night the plumber installed it. It was an upwardly mobile acquisition in the Manor and an obvious source of pride for its owners.

Our mothers seemed content to pull their grocery carts to the store, puff on mentholated Salem cigarettes, cook canned spaghetti and meatballs for their families, and float maraschino cherries in their Jell-O with a dollop of Cool Whip on top. Marshmallow Fluff was a luxury in those days. So was spray cheese, a popular item often served on Ritz crackers at Mahjong games.

The Eisners, a kosher family, enjoyed eating sausage pizza from Bob & Jacks at our house, but insisted on eating it on paper plates because our dishes weren't kosher. I know, kosher Jews eating pork sausage on paper plates at our house didn't make much sense. But few things did.

On Memorial Day each year, my parents hosted a backyard BBQ for their closest South Side friends and their families. Since it was also the weekend of my birthday, the BBQ frequently served a dual purpose.

My father enjoyed his role as the grill master. Unfortunately, however, he had neither the skills nor patience to let the coals grow hot enough after he'd added a large squirt of charcoal lighter fluid as a propellant. While the flames grew high enough to ignite another Chicago Fire, my father's always well-done hamburgers and hot dogs tasted more like lighter fluid than meat. But nobody ever seemed to complain, although some of us avoided his BBQ creations and opted instead for my mother's homemade potato salad and other side dishes supplied by our guests. (I have to give him credit, though: The only thing my father grilled exceedingly well were the toasted marshmallows he made for our S'mores.)

We children of the 1950s were raised as "happy, normal kids," and for the most part, we were. Most of us learned that our only way out from our side of the viaduct was to get a college education or to "marry well." (We had no idea what it meant to "marry well," as nobody we knew had any money.) Our parents wanted us to "do better." We heard that phrase a lot. It was our parents' mantra for "We have high hopes for you." We did our best to pursue our educations, but did we really "do better" than our parents?

It didn't take most of us long to understand the rhythm of life: we hung out with our Jewish friends in high school, screwed our brains out in college, avoided the draft by staying in college, earned our degrees, established our careers, got married (some got divorced, a few were gay and couldn't marry back then), watched our hair turn gray and/or fall out, gained weight, and learned that despite our higher aspirations, life for many of the baby boom generation consisted primarily of cellulite and chronic diseases.

Many in our generation of overeducated Manorites from the duplex ghetto became card-carrying depressives and contemplatives in high school, inspired in part by the pathos of Sylvia Plath. We thought we were intellectual because we read Ginsberg, Watts, Sartre, Camus, Thoreau, and Gibran in high school. We were existentialists. We practiced Transcendental Meditation and yoga. Some smoked pot and experimented with other illegal substances. Some obtained hippie identities at coffeehouses and used bookstores on 57th Street in Hyde Park on the University of Chicago campus, and others in Old Town on Chicago's Near North Side.

We learned about the Vietnam War and the lies perpetrated by our presidents and members of their cabinets. As a result, many of us became vocal anti-war protesters. Some became radicalized members of the SDS (Students for a Democratic Society). Others became conscientious objectors. Some marched and got tear-gassed. Others were arrested.

Like our parents, few of us reached the Promised Land. But unlike our parents, many of us grew educated enough to experience Waspy corporate backstabbing and other bureaucratic cruelties that resulted from our advanced degrees combined with basic Manor naiveté. Neither old money nor prep schoolers were we. We had the brains and the nose jobs to look Waspy, but not the country club memberships, preppy good looks, pedigrees, or DNA required to obtain the Greek paddles of the Tri Delts and others. Instead, we wore the viaduct as the amulet that adorned us wherever we went—like Hester Prynne's Scarlet A—as its soot attached itself to our souls.

Like our parents, we aspired to reach "Doing Betterville" after we left the realities of the Manor and college life behind. We soon came to learn that Doing Betterville is just an illusory myth created by Depression-Era and immigrant parents who hoped their children would one day shop up the escalator at Marshall Field's rather than downstairs, as they had to do, in the bargain basement.

And so, we did.

Some of us shopped at Bloomingdale's and Sachs and at chic little boutiques. After college, we spent ourselves silly, drove ourselves nuts, and mostly discovered that bliss was found in momentary absences of stress or diseases—and occasionally in a really good meal or a nice vacation. We earned our advanced degrees and we bought nice suburban homes with multiple bathrooms with real wooden vanities, three-car garages, and obscene mortgages. (As one dear, old Manor friend recently described them, "They're just bigger duplexes.") Some moved into exclusive communities promoted by ad agencies and populated with those of us who tried to avoid the possibility of losing our neighborhoods a second time.

Among my Manor acquaintances, two had nervous breakdowns, a few were closeted depressives, one overdosed on heroin, and one was a self-loathing girl known among Manor boys for her willingness to give blow jobs in the loading dock of the National Food Store before school started. Others were shoplifters and drug abusers. Several *should* have been in jail. One older neighbor boy placed my hand on the "hard thing" in his pants (I was still young enough to believe it was a piece of wood). Another neighbor boy, who said he always knew he was female, became transgender when she was in her fifties and her parents in their eighties. Before she transitioned, he was a married man with two sons. Sadly, she died a few years after transitioning but not before getting divorced from her wife, reconciling with her sons, and becoming happily engaged to a lovely man.

Some struggled with addictions of one type or another, including drugs, prescription painkillers, alcohol, nicotine, gambling, shopping, food, and sex. One neighbor and his son were "workaholics." Among my closest Manor friends, three of their offspring are dead from suicides, possibly influenced by genetics, family psychopathology, and/or drug habits.

As I think about this, the rate of mental illness in our neighborhood was probably not insignificant. A research study about addiction, depression, bipolar disorder, anxiety, trauma, reactive attachment disorder, and other personality disorders easily could have been conducted by sampling residents of the Manor. One neighbor up the street was known to have severe agoraphobia. Another neighbor experienced a reactive attachment disorder due to the emotional unavailability of her parents that led to a pattern of pursuing disappointing attachments throughout her life.

It is entirely possible that some recently returned soldiers in our neighborhood experienced post-traumatic stress disorder (PTSD). A few survivors of the Holocaust and war vets living nearby doubtlessly lived with traumatic brain injuries. Other possible causes: Genetics? Environmental factors? Research psychologists would have had a fertile sample of participants when evaluating the residents of our South Side neighborhood.

CHAPTER FIVE

Self-Segregation:
Germantown on the South Side of Chicago

When I was in college, I married my high school sweetheart. Stuart Low is without a doubt the best person that Bowen High School ever produced. Stu lived north of the viaduct and somehow, against all odds, he loved me in spite of my Manor ways (and in spite of the fact that I am not of German Jewish descent).

Stu, in all his wonderfulness, was the product of an extended family of depressive, obsessive-compulsive, and personality disordered German-Jewish WWII immigrants. His closest family members, very fortunately, were not victims of concentration camps. They'd been able to leave Germany just before things got really bad.

In fact, Stu's mother—at age eleven—and her father left their home in Frankfurt, Germany, on November 9, 1938, the historic day of Kristallnacht ("The Night of Broken Glass") during which Nazis looted and pillaged Jewish-owned businesses and synagogues throughout Germany. After having been advised by compassionate Christian neighbors to leave immediately, the Strauss family was sponsored to immigrate to America by a wealthy Episcopalian family in Cleveland, some of whose members had converted from Judaism. Stu's maternal grandmother left Frankfurt a month later after packing family treasures to be shipped to the U.S. The Nazis confiscated many of these, while less valuable heirlooms made their way safely to Cleveland. Stu's father's immediate family left Hamburg in 1935, and some other family members had already left for America.

While aware of the growing surge of power and hatred of Jews, Stu's immediate family did not suffer physically at the hands of Nazis. They suffered emotionally, however, and were left with a gnawing "survivor's guilt," knowing that they had survived while so many they knew had not. They suffered a second time too, knowing they'd left everything behind: their homes, jobs, synagogues, material goods, and language. They also left relatives and friends behind, those who failed to see the threat and those who lacked the means to leave. Their suffering manifested in depression, undisguised anger, and paranoia.

Once in America, virtually everything was new and different for them. They were forced to acquire a new language, adhere to new laws, learn new customs, and assume a new way of being. Some felt very much like outsiders and, at times, were treated poorly by their peers. Some attempted to blend in, while others fought assimilation by developing their own closed-off social networks.

Stu's family introduced me to a Jewish worldview that was far different from that of my family. Theirs was a subculture of otherness and alienation. Stu's family didn't worship or socialize with Jews who did not share their Holocaust narrative. Nor did they willingly socialize with non-Jews. They talked endlessly about money beyond the point of obsession. They shared paranoid ideations about how "others" might steal their money. And in some cases, they disowned their own children if they did not abide by their parents' wishes.

Stu's paternal Aunt Hilda was a money-obsessed, domineering woman who metaphorically "loaded, took aim, and shot" those whose values were not completely aligned with her own. A financially well-off tightwad, Aunt Hilda did not allow her daughter to own clothes that were not hand-me-downs. She did not allow her intelligent older granddaughter the right to attend the private college of her dreams because, she proclaimed, "You can get a good education at the state university, and I'm paying your tuition."

She later disinherited her adult son, Josh. Why? It was speculated that he and his non-German-Jewish wife maintained close Christian friendships and chose to live in Evanston, a racially integrated Chicago suburb, instead of the lily-white suburb of Aunt Hilda's choice. Josh was not even mentioned in the *Chicago Tribune* obituary when his 98-year-old mother died, an intentional omission by his estranged sister.

Unlike my family, Stu's family refused to eat pork, shellfish, or scavenger fish because of their adherence to kosher dietary laws. One of their Jewish neighbors, co-owner of a popular fish and seafood shack near the drawbridge on 95th Street and the Calumet River, produced the largest, most delectable fried shrimp imaginable. How could the Lows refuse their neighbor's frequent gifts of massive fried shrimp, especially when cartons of these golden treasures routinely were dropped off at their home, free of charge?

They couldn't.

So, the Lows revised their family's kosher practices to include the consumption of (free) shrimp. The consumption of lobster, crab, other crustaceans, and bottom-feeding fish remained verboten.

The Lows' favorite family pastime was playing cutthroat bridge. And woe be to their bridge partners if they failed to bid or play a hand correctly. Screaming, humiliating bridge games were the norm at Low family social gatherings.

The extended Low family assembled for Thanksgivings at a Hyde Park hotel banquet room for a roast beef dinner (Stu's great-uncle and father loathed turkey). Seemingly everybody eagerly awaited the end of the meal in order to set up card tables. The only "giving of thanks" occurred when bridge hands were bid and played correctly, and a family member wasn't eviscerated. Well-bid-and-played bridge hands were fondly remembered over the years, while losing hands long remained in family narratives, clearly intended to induce repeated shame in their bidders. There was only one year that bridge wasn't played, and that was the year we all experienced food poisoning and barely made it to the bathrooms in time. I steadfastly refused to learn how to play bridge after witnessing so many traumatizing "Thanksgiving" bridge games.

Stu and I began a new tradition of alternating Thanksgiving celebrations with my family and their close friends (traditionally American in every sense) and the Lows until we moved away and created our own Thanksgiving celebrations, none of which ever included bridge games or roast beef.

Generally, when their children married non-German Jews, we "outsider" spouses were considered tainted second-class citizens. Once, after turning twenty-one, I ordered a cocktail at a restaurant during a Low family dinner. From that moment on, Stu's mother concluded that I had a drinking problem. She graciously offered me opportunities to fuel my imagined "alcoholism" at future dinners out. I never consumed another cocktail in her presence because of the obvious delight she derived from her snap and misguided judgment. Stu's mother frequently bought bottles of Amaretto at Costco for her non-German-Jewish son-in-law. Clearly, he was also perceived by his mother-in-law to have a drinking problem. The irony was that Stu's father (who in later years managed the liquor department at Marshall Field's at the Water Tower Place after spending most of his adult life managing the Hyde Park Co-Op) enjoyed a nightcap after almost every dinner. *His* obvious pleasure was never questioned or judged.

The German Jews of the South Side clustered in Hyde Park and South Shore neighborhoods, although some of their poorer brethren moved to the Manor. My ancestors migrated—with very little money or material wealth—from Russia/Ukraine and Lithuania during the pogroms of the late 19th century. Most landed in the Jewish ghetto around Maxwell Street and later moved to the West Side and South Side; some moved North.

German Jews tended to regard the Eastern European Jews as less cultured. To Stu's parents and their cohorts, non-German Jews were consciously kept outside of their social circles. And, as I would eventually learn, I was part of that excluded group.

The only notable exception to the Low family German Jewish rule of exclusion occurred when Stu's wealthy industrialist great uncle—who left Germany in the 1920s and died before Stu and I dated—married Martha, a Methodist woman from Nebraska whom he'd met on a cruise ship. Martha was a lovely and accomplished woman, and Stu's extended family fawned over her. I often wondered why, as she wasn't Jewish, let alone a German Jew.

As I soon learned, Martha inherited her late husband's estate, reportedly worth a fortune. And pity the Lows should Martha choose to leave the entirety of her late husband's estate to her gentile Nebraska relatives and not to them. So, they curried favor to reassure Martha that she was a venerated member of the Low clan. Martha was not stupid and I'm fairly certain she understood their motives.

As Stu and I became more serious, his family did their very best to subtly and not so subtly ply me with various microaggressions. When Oma, Stu's maternal grandmother, visited his family's apartment, she and Stu's mother frequently conversed in German while in my presence, knowing of course that I had no idea what they were saying. Oma maintained a malevolent little twinkle in her eye during these interactions, which usually took place in the Low's kitchen when other family members weren't around.

Dinner discussions at their home always centered on reminiscences of Low family summer vacations, personal anecdotes, and stories about people they knew. I do not recall the Lows inquiring about my family, my background, or my interests. It became very clear they had no interest in me.

At one family Sabbath dinner, hosted by Stu's Great Aunt Mildred, we gathered around the Sabbath candlesticks, Kiddush cup (wine goblet), and challah bread on the table. As Aunt Mildred prepared to light the Sabbath candles, she explained the Sabbath prayers in heavily accented English: "For Martha and Debbie, who are not of our faith." I elbowed Stu in the ribs and whispered, "Doesn't she know I'm Jewish?" Stu responded, "Well yes, but you're not a *German* Jew." (It didn't matter if I was a German or Russian Jew; the prayers were still the same!)

Turns out neither was Aunt Mildred's non-Jewish daughter-in-law, married to her only child, Albert, who was encouraged to never set foot in her Hyde Park apartment. And so, she didn't. Now long deceased, Aunt Mildred would be horrified to know that her beloved grandson is a convicted pedophile who recently completed a lengthy sentence in a California prison for molesting boys he had coached. Aunt Mildred would probably attribute her grandson's criminal behavior to his having a gentile mother.

The Lows were not at all happy that Stu called and wrote to me every single day of their lengthy summer vacation, scheduled just after our high school graduation and shortly before he left for Oberlin College in Ohio. When Stu transferred to the University of Illinois his sophomore year to reunite with me, get engaged, and ultimately get married as an undergraduate, it was the beginning of the Low's family nightmare.

One of the standout photos in our wedding album features a close-up of Stu's teary-eyed mother tightly grasping a Kleenex as she and her dour husband accompanied a happily smiling Stu up the aisle to the huppa (wedding canopy).

After graduating from college, Stu and I moved back to Chicago, to Hyde Park. We lived with the Lows for six weeks while a nearby apartment was being prepared for us. They allowed us to share Stu's twin bed. Nine months after our wedding, his mother had not yet accepted the fact that her son was a married man and, as such, was enjoying intimate relations with his wife in his childhood bed... *in their apartment.* There was a lot of hovering outside our bedroom door during our stay.

Trust me, it was a *long* six weeks.

We attempted to establish our lives in peace after we moved to our one-bedroom apartment on the 11th floor of an apartment building on 51st Street in Hyde Park just east of the IC tracks (Illinois Central RR, later known as METRA). Oma, Stu's maternal grandmother, lived less than a block from us. She noticed when I moved a begonia plant from our living room window to the windowsill in our master bedroom, and called to ask why I would do such a thing. Stu's parents, who lived four blocks away, requested our presence *every* Friday night for Sabbath dinner. We refused to make that commitment because we weren't observant and we also wanted to spend some Friday nights alone, with my family, and sometimes with our Chicago area friends. Guess who was blamed for that?

To "welcome" us to Hyde Park, Aunt Hilda—also a Hyde Park resident—"graced" us with a visit to our apartment. Within minutes of her arrival, she opened our master bedroom closet door and proclaimed, "Debbie, you have too many clothes." My wardrobe at that time consisted of the two pairs of faded bell-bottom jeans that I wore throughout college, several T-shirts, two denim work shirts, and three dresses that I was required to wear at my new job at Marshall Field's. Stu's mother, who was also present, remained mute and offered no support to this twenty-two-year-old. Nor did she offer any explanation after the incident. Did she agree with Aunt Hilda? Or did she lack the backbone to challenge this intrusive, opinionated woman? Whatever the explanation, my mother-in-law's lack of support was noted, and quite frankly, not forgotten.

Stu and I moved away from Chicago within a year, not only to attend graduate school but also to regain our sanity.

Like most Southsiders in the late 1960s, the Lows moved from their home after Blacks began moving into their neighborhood. They first moved back to Hyde Park to be close to Stu's father's workplace. Later, they moved north to a high-rise on Lake Shore Drive and Irving Park Road. They finally left Chicago for a retirement community in Orange County, California.

Over the years, Stu's father retained his distinct German accent along with his strong German-Jewish identity. Although deeply aware of his family's Holocaust narrative and the challenges experienced by his fellow German Jews, he did not appear to have empathy for other races or nationalities. Shortly after their move to California, he displayed his true colors at a restaurant in Newport Beach.

Our waiter wore a nametag that visibly stated, "Carlos." After we were seated, he politely greeted us and inquired about our beverage preferences. Stu's father looked at him and said, "I'd like coffee, Juan." Our waiter flushed and returned with our drinks. A few moments later, Carlos returned to take our food orders. My father-in-law said, "Juan,

I'd like the fish of the day." This time, Carlos looked a bit rattled but said nothing. Stu's father smirked.

We—including our then ten-year-old son, David—witnessed this exchange. I was fuming, particularly because my father-in-law was modeling overtly racist behavior in front of his impressionable grandson. I looked at my father-in-law and said softly, "I know you're new to California. You may not realize that there are a lot of Hispanic people living here. You should be more respectful to people of other backgrounds."

Apparently, no one had ever challenged Stu's father, the family patriarch, before. He glared at me after I commented on his behavior. Stu and his mother refused to make eye contact. David played with his Transformer, thankfully oblivious to the growing tension at our table.

After Carlos served our food, Stu's mother filled the silence with insipid banter. We learned about their new experiences in Laguna Hills. The patter continued except for Stu's father, who remained silent as he continued to stare angrily at me.

In fact, he refused to speak to me for the duration of our visit. What's more, he never again spoke to me on the phone when I answered. He had his wife place all of their calls to our home. Only after I turned the phone over to Stu would his father pick up an extension.

What my father-in-law did accomplish was to add fuel to the fire. On one subsequent visit to our home, he placed his sweaty baseball cap on the head of a terracotta statue of a Native American woman displayed on our family room hearth. He said he didn't like the statue because it looked like the Virgin Mary. I went to our utility room cabinet and found two sticky hooks to place inside our guest room closet. I returned to the family room to inform all present that these hooks were now available to hang caps and other items when not in use. Stu's father continued to hang his cap on our statue on that trip and whenever they visited.

In August 1991, Stu's parents planned a vacation at a resort near Lake of the Ozarks, Missouri, for the extended family. We were to fly to Chicago and drive with Stu's parents to the resort where we would meet up with Stu's sister and her family who lived near St. Louis.

At that time, my father was close to death and living in a skilled nursing facility in Tempe, Arizona, adjacent to my mother's apartment. As the family trip grew nearer, I told Stu that I was feeling increasingly anxious about possibly being stranded in rural Missouri and far from a major airport should we be called back to Arizona.

We left for Chicago with my mother's blessing. With growing concerns about my father's rapidly declining health, however, I suggested that Stu, David, and I remain in Chicago while the remainder of the family enjoyed their trip to Missouri. I knew we could easily catch a flight back to Phoenix from Chicago if the need arose.

Stu's father was furious that I had scuttled their plans for a family vacation, despite knowing about my father's increasingly fragile condition. Stu and I strongly encouraged them to continue with their plans, so they proceeded to meet Stu's sister and her family at the resort while we remained at their apartment in Chicago. My father, who at that time suffered from painful gastrointestinal ascites and esophageal varices from liver failure, died a few weeks later. Stu's father never forgave me for ruining their family vacation plans.

Six years later, without any obvious suffering, and several days before his seventy-fifth birthday, my father-in-law died in his sleep from a heart attack. We had planned to celebrate his special birthday in California with the family. Instead, we quickly repacked our luggage for a Chicago funeral.

Years later, Stu's mother also died from a heart attack—or possibly from a broken heart—a few weeks before she was to witness her daughter's son marry a Catholic woman five years older than him. Stu's parents would be horrified to know that their three grandchildren, respectively, married a never-practicing half-Jew, a Catholic, and a Methodist. None of their grandchildren are religious, although all were raised Jewish.

Stu's mother had grieved long and hard about losing her son to an outsider. She shared her unhappy feelings with her husband, her daughter, and others in her close circle. This went on for years. Stu was clearly, and quite unfairly, stuck in the middle of his unhappy parents and his disgusted wife. Peace was realized only after their deaths, although their ghosts are never easy to suppress and still haunt me from time to time.

Chapter Six

No Exodus from Insanity

S tu interviewed at a variety of universities for an academic position during his doctoral dissertation process. He received four job offers to become an assistant professor of economics: from Temple University in Philadelphia, the University of North Carolina at Greensboro, the University of Texas at Austin, and Arizona State University in Tempe. After an in-depth review of each of the offers, Stu accepted the offer from Arizona State, and we moved in 1979 in the midst of the monsoon season. It proved helpful to the salvation of our marriage and our psyches to be far away from our families.

Today, the Phoenix metropolitan area is booming with semiconductor manufacturing plants and planned communities comprised mostly of faux Spanish white stucco homes and red tile roofs as far as the eye can see. These "stick and stucco" homes (as we refer to them) are quite unlike our boxy Manor duplexes that were mostly built of solid brick. Our more spacious, red-tiled Arizona homes are routinely constructed of two-by-fours for structure, Styrofoam for insulation, chicken wire to hold it all in place, and a thin layer of stucco to justify the cost and attempt to make them look Southwestern. It's not entirely inconceivable that our neighborhood could blow away in a monsoon storm.

The sociology in the Phoenix metropolitan area is distinctly different from that on either side of the viaducts of my youth. In Arizona, we live with a significant population of white Christians, Native Americans, Mexicans, and Mormons. There are relatively few Jews or Blacks, at least in our neighborhood. We have a significant population of Chicago ex-pats and Midwestern "snowbirds." We're always surprised when we see a mezuzah on a doorpost in our Arizona neighborhood. Our Arizona house is conspicuously void of Christmas lights during the holiday season, but I am known to go overboard with Chanukah decorations to make our presence known!

There are few reminders here of our South Side past, although every now and then, we get surprised by a few relics. Almost two decades ago, for instance, the Pincuses (our neighbors across the street in the Manor) phoned my mom to let her know they'd purchased a condo on "the other side of the river" up in Scottsdale. Simply by living in Scottsdale, they regarded themselves as Very Important People. This meant they never crossed the Salt River to see us. In Arizona, the Salt River is the natural division between north and south, much like the viaduct on Chicago's South Side. Those who live south of the Salt River are essentially viewed as equivalent to those who lived south of the viaduct. You can guess where we live. It is no surprise that the Pincuses opted for the North Side.

Even after living in Arizona for more than forty years, in my heart I remain a South Sider. I was born there in 1952 to a sickly mother and a struggling father, each yearning for a life without loneliness. Try as they might, mother's health deteriorated, and father continuously struggled in all aspects of his life.

I was raised at a time when we begged coins to buy penny candy from Benny the kosher butcher, the shrunken Russian immigrant who we all knew made more money selling candy than from killing and selling his skinny little chickens. When the Good Humor truck came rolling down our street on sultry summer evenings, I was given the option of either no ice cream or a Dixie cup filled with Walgreen's ice cream, since we couldn't afford the tantalizing icy confections doled out from the freezers of that beautiful white truck.

On summer nights, we chased DDT trucks on our bikes and

enshrouded ourselves in the clouds of poison meant to kill mosquitoes, not children. Our dirty little fingers pushed fireflies inside Miracle Whip jars with lids punctured by the tips of Bic pens to let them breathe. We fed them grass and once I fed them our cocker spaniel's Alpo. They lost their glow after that.

In the summertime, Marla and I sang "Que Sera, Sera" for hours on end and we ate green grapes on our front stoops. Stevie, Marky, and I made go-karts with the wheels from our roller skates nailed onto plywood. We never made it down the driveway before they broke apart.

The summer that I turned six, Stevie's younger sister gouged out the hair and scalp on some of her older sister's dolls with their father's Phillips screwdriver. Later that same summer, Stevie kicked in part of their living room wall during a fit of rage. My mother said it was a good thing it wasn't the common wall in their duplex.

The kids on my block watched nighttime summer skies to the east become a radiant shade of orange created by the nightshift workers pouring slag at the nearby steel mills. None of us knew we were living—and for some, eventually dying—in a cancer–causing environment.

Most summer nights we played tag, statue maker, dodgeball, and red rover, and rode our bikes while fireflies and mosquitoes filled the hot Chicago skies. Jump rope, jacks, hopscotch, and Double Dutch were also among our favorite activities. In 1959, both Barbie Dolls and hula hoops became the rage. Stuie Harknesses' younger sister Peggy was dubbed the hula hoop queen of our street. She went on to become a high school cheerleader and eventually a senior cheerleader for the Orlando Magic.

As kids, we roller skated with our clamp-on skates, our skate keys secure on the lanyards around our necks. We skated for hours up and down the concrete driveway of our neighbors who boasted the only smoothly paved driveway on our block.

Bike riding was clearly our preferred mode of transportation. But there were known hazards: 1) freshly-edged lawns that our bike tires would get stuck in, inevitably leading to bloodied knees and elbows treated with mercurochrome; 2) unobservant children who rode their bikes into the paths of drivers; and 3) sticker bushes that impaled Marla when she lost control of her bike. One family, the Meremans, had four children who were continually injured from biking, falling off their roof, starting fires—and assorted other "accidents." Fortunately, Marla's mom served as our Brennan Avenue health care provider. Her first aid kit was always well stocked.

Marla and I were either social misfits or social scientists, depending on one's point of view. Our mothers plotted together to find ways to keep us busy during the long, hot, boring summers. One summer they enrolled us in the daytime Luella School camp led by a woman named Sunny. Sunny did a fine job directing activities for average, well-adjusted neighborhood kids to keep them engaged and off the streets. But not us. Marla and I lasted all of three days and concluded that we had zero interest in playing softball and other organized team sports. During craft time, we made lanyards to hold our roller skate keys. After that, we were done.

The next summer, our mothers enrolled us in Girl Scout Day Camp. We rode a yellow school bus from the Manor to East Side neighborhoods to a park near Wolf Lake on the Illinois/Indiana border. Neither Marla nor I would even try to relate to girls who had surnames like Polkowscowitz, Mrzerich, and Kecichovic, who lived in flats near the steel mills. We believed we had nothing in common with them. The counselors provided us with cartons of warm milk or sometimes red, sticky-sweet juice (called "Bug Juice") from large jugs. Marla and I clung to each other and held back from engaging in Girl Scout activities. This time, we lasted four days.

Another summer, our mothers tried again, this time enrolling us in swimming classes at the Chicago Vocational High School's indoor pool. Marla and I complained that the pool smelled like body odor. To make matters worse, a layer of grease floated on the surface of the water. We were appalled by the stench and the thought of swimming in a place that made its male students swim nude. We were afraid we'd get pregnant. Our vehement protests notwithstanding, we were forced to remain for an entire week.

Just where were we comfortable? At each other's homes, with other neighborhood friends, and just doing whatever we wanted to do with people we knew. The reality was, Marla and I were extremely shy. We hid behind our shyness by avoiding people who were unlike us.

Sometimes we made dandelion necklaces on the O'Shannons' lawn and played with Mimi, their toy poodle, who also served as Dan O'Shannon's personal "cigar-butt canine ashtray" where he'd flick his ashes. Dan was a good sport, often filling in as the required 10th man for a Jewish minyan. God bless Mr. O'Shannon!

On most summertime evenings, the men on our block pulled their webbed lawn chairs over to Herby Fine's driveway to listen to my dad's raunchy jokes and Natty Lerner's stories. Our mothers carried their lawn chairs over to Bertha's driveway where they mostly bragged about their kids and complained about their husbands.

In those days, our front doors were never locked, and our neighbors walked in whenever they pleased—morning, noon, and night. You never knew just who would walk in.

One night, the summer that I was five, my parents went over for pizza and Coke at our duplex neighbors' half of the house. Only they didn't tell me about it, probably because they thought I'd want to tag along. They put me to bed and waited until I fell asleep. For some reason, I woke up and called out for my mother. No response. I called out again and still nobody answered. I was really scared and pulled the bedsheet over my head. The next thing I remember was a lot of screaming, followed by a big bang.

A Black man (this occurred many years before our neighborhood became integrated) entered our unlocked front door and was walking up the stairs toward my bedroom at precisely the moment my father came to check on me. All hell broke loose! The intruder jumped back down the stairs, and ran past my dad through our living room and into our kitchen. He slammed the door behind him as he ran down into our basement. My dad locked him in the basement, ran back into the living room, and rammed his fist into the common duplex wall. That action caused our duplex neighbor to investigate the thud. By the end of the evening, several of our neighbors—along with Chicago policemen—were gathered in our living room. The intruder, however, escaped by breaking one of our basement windows and hightailed it out of the house. This whole thing was an unprecedented occurrence as far as we knew.

Ajax, a house painter and jack-of-all-trades, was the only man of color any of our neighbors knew who worked in the neighborhood. The consensus, rightly or wrongly, was that it was Ajax who entered our home. We'll never know because he was never seen again on Brennan Avenue.

We lived with my father's implanted fist mark in the common duplex wall, a constant reminder of a very scary night in our little Manor hamlet. After that, everyone kept their doors open, but only until dinnertime. After dinner, all the doors and windows on our block were tightly locked and chained.

Chapter Seven

Scary Times and Flying Milk Bottles

*It is only in our darkest hours that we may discover the true strength of
the brilliant light within ourselves that can never, ever, be dimmed.*

– Doe Zantamata

Actually, things were already scary in my house long before that
night.

After four years of marriage, my birth represented new life and
hope for my parents, Eddie and Iris. I was a colicky baby. People have
told me that I never stopped crying until just after my first birthday.
I'm not sure why I stopped crying then.

I learned at a very young age that my primary role in our little family
was to be an emotional buffer for my mom, to help her construct a
fantasy far better than the frequent verbal abuse she experienced from
my father and his oldest sister. My mother and I watched my father
lose his business and barely avert a bankruptcy before his thirty-fifth
birthday. My father's temper grew disproportionately larger as money
grew increasingly scarcer.

Mom told me on multiple occasions that my father rarely displayed
anger during their courtship. She said she never would have married
him had she known about the prevalence of mental illness in his
family. My father's oldest sister was a miserable bully. His middle

sister was locked away in a state mental hospital in Kankakee, Illinois, after receiving a diagnosis of schizophrenia. While in the hospital, she endured electroshock treatments and a frontal lobotomy. As it turns out, she was the nicest of the three siblings.

To survive my father's frequent verbal rages, my mother resided in a cognitive memory bank of her idyllic childhood and her supportive and loving parents and a near-perfect sister. When my dad was at work, her alternative universe included hours of phone conversations with her friends, shopping trips to 95th Street with Bertha, soap operas and Mahjong games.

Once he came home, however, her obligation was to feed him, fetch for him ("Iris, bring me a glass of milk." "Where is my pipe? Get it for me!"), and to obey his every command. Not once did I hear a word of thanks or appreciation uttered from his lips. My mother's servitude was a direct result of my father's toxic masculinity and lack of respect for women, especially his wife. My father graciously allowed my mom to play Mahjong on some evenings, but only if he had something to occupy his time.

Other than my father and his horrific oldest sister (whom he called "Bloody Mary"), everyone else who knew my mom loved her sweetness, kindness, and gentle good nature. My mom rarely wore a blouse that wasn't old or slacks that fit properly. She never wore makeup except for occasional lipstick. She wore tiny orthopedic shoes on her size four and a half feet. A weekly indulgence was her Saturday morning visit to her hair stylist, Sue, at the beauty parlor on 100th Street for a wash, trim and set to try to tame her curly red locks. (And, for a chance to catch up on Manor gossip and to glimpse at the tabloids while under the dryer.)

Bloody Mary lived north of the viaduct. She looked down her nose at Manorites, especially my grandparents. She was angry that my grandfather, the dentist, didn't set my dad up in a small business as she had demanded. My grandparents assured her that they never intended to underwrite my father's business endeavors. Smart thing for them.

Bloody Mary never helped her younger brother either. She became very wealthy as a result of inheriting the assets of her late husband, a tavern owner and real estate investor in mostly Black neighborhoods on the South Side.

My aunt was cruel to members of our family. When I was four, my parents were invited to her South Shore apartment for dinner with extended family members. While my father sat with other guests at her dining room table, my mother and I were relegated to her bedroom because I was not allowed to make an appearance. I remember sitting on the floor in her bedroom. I also remember my mother's unhappiness at being locked away from the other adults. My mother was being punished by Bloody Mary for not finding a babysitter for me.

One day, when I was in sixth grade, I was on my way home from school when I noticed Bloody Mary's car parked in front of our house. I walked in on the scene of my aunt excoriating my mother for God-knows-what reasons. My mother looked daunted and overwhelmed. My father was at work at the time.

After listening for a few minutes, I told my aunt, "It's time for you to leave." She looked at me and growled, "What did you say, young lady?" I told her that I didn't like the way she was speaking to my mother and said it would be best for her to leave our house.

Much to our surprise, she stood abruptly and seethed, "Your mother didn't raise you to respect your elders." I quickly replied, "I was raised to respect *decent* people of all ages." She left in a huff. Later that year, when I received a check in the mail from her for Chanukah, I tore it up and gave the pieces to my mother. Fortunately for me, my dad found the whole thing to be quite amusing.

Bloody Mary's daughter Raquel was married to a Rexall pharmacist. My parents took me to his drugstore to purchase a Timex watch as a Chanukah gift for me. I selected one with a gold-rimmed face and a thin black velveteen band to replace my broken Cinderella watch. We were all happy with the new watch, especially since it was purchased at a deep discount.

A couple of months later, while baking cookies at one of our Girl Scout meetings in the basement of the Manor Community Church, a nasty girl in my troop stole my recently-acquired Timex watch. I had placed it in an unlocked cubby space. We were Girl Scouts, after all, and we should have been able to trust one another. At the end of the meeting after the other Scouts left, I revealed the theft to my mother—a co-leader of our troop along with Marla's mom. My mother panicked because she knew my father would be furious. She told me she was afraid he would call the homes of each of the Girl Scouts, demanding retribution. She swore me to secrecy.

Before my father came home from work, my mom phoned stores in the area and discovered that the Steinway Drug Store on 87th Street and Stony Island carried the exact same Timex watch. While my dad was at work the next day, my mother and I rode the Jeffery Boulevard bus to 87th Street. Then we walked almost a mile through a snowstorm to purchase the substitute watch. My father never learned about the theft or our deception. We did whatever we could to avoid his temper tantrums.

I imagine that as a result of the stress of living with my father's severe mood swings, explosive tantrums, and frequent threats of divorce (many in my presence), as well as being within striking range of Bloody Mary, my Mother became an anxiety-stricken, uncontrolled diabetic by her mid-30s. She spent too many days in too many hospital beds during my youth, with illnesses primarily related to uncontrolled diabetes.

When I was almost nine, Mom gave birth to a full-term stillborn baby boy. Shortly thereafter, she had a radical hysterectomy. My mother never spoke about her loss, but she and my father took me to the Museum of Science and Industry to view fetuses in jars, an admittedly bizarre but well-intentioned attempt to help me understand what had grown inside her body, month after month.

The times I spent alone with my father when my mother was hospitalized were frightening because in her absence, his anger was directed at me. On one occasion, he offered to make me a peanut butter and jelly sandwich, one of my favorites. My father, who rarely spent time in the kitchen, decided that both sides of the bread needed to be slathered first with a thick layer of butter before he added the peanut butter and jelly.

I took one bite out of the sandwich and gagged loudly.

"What did you put on the bread? It tastes terrible!"

He glared at me and told me about the buttered bread.

"Mom doesn't make it this way!!!"

I set the sandwich down and refused to take another bite. My father glared at me. "Eat it," he commanded. But I wouldn't touch it. He yelled again. "Take another bite. Now!" I took a tiny bite and gagged again. I started crying and refused to eat. We sat at the kitchen table at a stalemate until he finally gave up and stormed off. When she came home, I told my mother what happened. Fortunately, after that, she decided I would be much happier (and safer) staying with her sister's family whenever she had to be in the hospital.

Mom said we couldn't hold my dad responsible for his crudeness or raging fits. "He can't help himself," she told me, "because his mother died when he was nine and his father didn't have any interest in raising a young boy." My father purportedly was "raised on the streets" without parental guidance, was frequently in trouble, and was an unmotivated, under-achieving student.

What apparently helped provide my father with an identity and a sense of place and purpose was his service in the Army Air Force as a Private First-Class during WWII. While my father's reputation was that of a rebellious and troubled teenager, four years of military service provided much-needed structure and discipline for this rowdy young man. For him and for so many others, military service was a rite of passage into manhood, a time when he learned the importance of rules and when he experienced the brotherly camaraderie of his fellow soldiers. The fact that these young men fought in a war they believed in for a country they loved added to the significance of their experiences.

He was both a gunner and an aerial photographer on bombing missions. Our basement walls in the Manor were lined with photographs that he had taken of incredible mushroom clouds. The beautiful cloud formations concealed the devastation of the bombs they dropped and the destruction they wreaked on Italian targets. As a child, I had no understanding of what truth lay beneath these awesome mushroom cloud formations.

My dad would talk almost endlessly about the war and his service. He maintained strong friendships with a few of his war buddies, a couple of whom we went to visit. I remember that he and his buddies exchanged holiday cards each year.

I'm not sure if my father's Jewish identity was affected in any way by the fact that his unit was bombing Axis Fascists in Italy who were aligned with the Nazis. After he retired, he created elaborate scrapbooks of printed materials about WWII that he photocopied as a volunteer at the Holocaust Museum in Skokie and brought home. The time he spent there reinforced his obsessive fascination with the war, destruction, and the ultimate victory over the Nazis.

He spoke of his basic training at an airbase in Pocatello, Idaho, and his intense passion for a young woman he met in town. Unfortunately for my father, the object of his desire was Mormon, and her parents were not at all interested in having a Jewish son-in-law. If he had remained at that base, I suspect my father would have converted to Mormonism, knowing how little he valued his Jewish heritage. But he was soon sent to Italy. Once he was deployed there, he said he saw Pope Pius XII pass by in a motorcade. He liked to boast that he'd received a "personal blessing" from him as the motorcade drove by. My father, never knowing that Pope Pius XII was a notorious anti-Semite, went to his grave believing he'd been individually blessed by a saintly man.

Another story I heard often was about a plane crash my father was in when he was stationed in Pocatello. Fortunately, nobody died and my father was left with a broken jaw that was wired shut for some time. I think it's entirely possible that he sustained a traumatic brain injury during the crash, which may have contributed to his intense chronic anger issues that surfaced a few years later and persisted throughout the remainder of his life. My father continued to obsess about his war experiences and took solace in his scrapbooks and photographs. He was most peaceful during those times, and at times when he was curating his collection of stamps. To this day, I still remember those stamps that contained artwork, flowers, and costumes.

The rest of the time, however, he raged. He raged at home and at work about various slights that he perceived. He raged on *every one* of our vacations, mostly road trips that always started with my mother suffering a severe bout of anxiety, largely due to her insecurity and forgetfulness. On every road trip, we packed up the car—including my trusty pillow I'd named "Montgomery"—and left our home with a sense of excitement and anticipation. I lay across the back seat of the car, my head on Montgomery, covered with a blanket and entertained by an assortment of books, magazines, dolls, and toys. In looking back, I can now see that *every one* of those road trips derailed about fifty miles away from our home.

It always went something like this:

My mother uttered, "Shoot," under her breath. "What's wrong?" my father queried.

"Nothing," she responded. And then, she clammed up for another ten miles or so. And, sighed heavily. And repeatedly.

"What is it?" my father asked, with growing agitation.

Here is where my mother's answers varied. "I think I left the iron plugged in." Or "I left the oven on." Or "I forgot to lock the door." Or "I left the television on." One time she said, "I don't know if I turned the water off in the kitchen."

With incredible anger and frustration, my father would turn the car around and drive home, all the while seething. My mother would remain silent. I knew better than to open my mouth.

And here's what we found: no irons were ever left plugged in. No oven or television or faucet was left on. The doors were always locked. After checking everything out and taking a bathroom break at home, we'd leave on our road trip for a second time but now in an increased state of stress and anxiety. Whatever initial excitement I'd felt about the trip was gone. The car ride was silent. The anger was palpable.

I wanted to be anywhere but in that car with them. The good news was that by the time we stopped for a lunch break—generally after my father refused to read the map or listen to my mother's directions and inevitably missed the exit—the anger would lift and the mood in the car improved somewhat. My father, in spite of what he believed about himself, proved to be fallible. He just never admitted it and we knew better than to point it out.

Another significant event that I recall vividly and will never forget occurred in our Manor duplex. While seated at the kitchen table, I watched my father forcefully throw a mostly-filled glass milk bottle at the common duplex kitchen wall because he was angry that my mother was on the phone when he came home from work and didn't have his dinner waiting for him on the table. To say it was traumatizing is an understatement.

That event—complete with milk dripping down the wall, puddles on the kitchen table and floor, broken shards of glass, and blood covering my father's hand after he picked up pieces of glass from our kitchen table—occurred more than sixty years ago. The memory of that scene and of my father's rage is still very fresh in my mind. To this day, I cringe or freeze when I hear loud, angry voices.

My father broke laws as he saw fit. One year, in anticipation of Chanukah, I requested a chemistry set as my main gift. My dad looked at several different chemistry sets and determined that the "best set" was relatively more expensive than the others. So, he switched price tags, making the priciest set more affordable. When presenting me with this gift, he boasted about how he switched price tags. I remember having a sick feeling in the pit of my stomach—especially knowing that as a former small storeowner himself, he would have been furious if someone had done that in his shop.

In laymen's terms, my father was an emotionally ill, personality-disordered rebellious boy stuck in a man's body. He had toddler-like temper tantrums when things didn't go his way. He was a narcissist, a rule-breaker, a bigot, and a bully. I think my mother loved him in the way she may have loved an injured baby bird or an abandoned puppy. He frequently embarrassed us. I know she missed the kind of life she had hoped to share with him. But she never missed his raging anger after he died.

As a youngster in the summers, I fled from my father's weekly Sunday morning meltdowns by leaving our house and heading over to Marla's. She and her parents knew what was going on in my house because they—like all our other neighbors—could hear through open windows my father's ranting. By Sunday afternoon, my father typically cooled off, after which my parents would attempt to make things right by taking me on much-hated family car rides. Most of the time, there was total silence in the car. Often, we'd end up at some discount store where my father attempted to demonstrate his love with age-appropriate gifts. As I write this, I am sitting next to my first AM transistor radio, a Mitsubishi in a brown leather case acquired on one such outing.

Other Sundays—post-meltdown—we'd head on excursions with our family friends, the Maslows, or with my friend Wilma and her parents. In the summertime, my parents and Wilma's parents would occasionally rent a motel room on South Shore Drive so we could swim in the motel pool. Interestingly, while the Maslows were fully aware of my father's raging behaviors, Wilma was never aware that my father battled demons.

In first grade, my teacher, Mrs. Sullivan, phoned my mother to inquire why I was such a "little worrywart." My mother innocently replied that she had no idea that I was worried or what I was worried about. My mother also couldn't understand why I wouldn't invite my classmates home after school. Or why I avoided being at home when I was in high school. Probably out of a sense of self-preservation, she couldn't bring herself to comprehend how life with my dad had affected me.

Anxiety was my closest companion, frequently made more acute after one of my father's uproars. I occasionally "froze" on tests and later developed acute math anxiety. In sixth grade, I once froze while taking a test. I couldn't remember the answer to a question that I had understood the night before. I whispered to Marky for help. Frustrated, he told the teacher that I was cheating, which led to an embarrassing confrontation with my teacher and a long break in my friendship with Marky.

As a teenager, I grew weary of my father's extreme mood swings, misogynistic jokes, and racist diatribes. My mother and I still walked on eggshells around him because we never knew which version of my father—Dr. Jekyll or Mr. Hyde—would come through the door at night. I didn't want to be around him. I wanted him to leave so we could attain some stability and sanity in our home.

Conventional wisdom in those days underscored the importance of keeping marriages intact for the "good" of the children. Based on my experiences, I strongly believed—and still do—that children should not be subjected to the insane moods and erratic behaviors of an unstable parent. It is unhealthy for children to learn that they can't trust their parents. My father was highly combustible, and my sweet, fragile mother lacked the ability to protect either of us. Just who could I trust? As it turned out, I was thrust into the role of "responsible adult" at an early age, a role I never should have been required to assume as a child.

Sarcasm and cynicism became my strongest coping strategies and defense mechanisms as a teen. I earned a reputation for making funny but snarky comments, many directed at people I found contemptuous—entitled, obnoxious, spoiled, snobby, selfish, and mean-spirited people of all ages. Over the years I have worked hard to smooth out my sharp edges and discover my kinder self.

It's probably no surprise that I became a psychotherapist after spending such an anxious life with imperfect family members, friends, and neighbors. Therapy taught me that identifying one's vulnerabilities and speaking one's truth are among the most healing forms of self-care. (That and trying not to bludgeon others when you're ready to speak your truth.)

My training as a therapist helped me understand the underlying pathologies of my father's rage; self-interest; crude comments about women, racial/ethnic minorities and gay people; emotional abuse; and his rule-breaking behaviors. Once I recognized these traits, I was finally able to transition from hating him to pitying him for never seeking diagnoses or treatment for his mental illnesses. At the same time, though, I never stopped hating many of his disgusting behaviors. (And I especially pitied my mother for enduring my father's emotional abuse for forty-three years as a classic codependent.)

Sadly, the effects of his mental illnesses were like a tsunami, deeply impacting my mother and me, and affecting his relationships with neighbors, friends, and co-workers. For example, the wife of my father's childhood best friend would not allow her husband to see my father because of my Dad's foul mouth. Other close friends' spouses barely tolerated my father because of the way he treated my mother and others.

Fortunately, my training as a therapist and my own personal counseling provided me with the ability to make meaning out of his mental illnesses.

I further healed by mindfully seeking healthy and respectful relationships as I grew into a teenager and later as an adult. At age eighteen, when I left my parents' home for college, I consciously vowed that I would *never* be in a relationship with a man like my father. When I met Stu, I quickly found that he was the antithesis of my father. Stu was kind, warm, polite, and respectful. He was also very wise and funny. While he carried his own emotional baggage from his family of origin, his goodness shined through.

In addition to Marla, my closest friendship in life came at age fifteen when I met Joan in our sophomore geometry class. Joan and I frequently hung out with other friends, but the bond between the two of us was formed fast and has lasted more than fifty years. Joan's family home was calm and peaceful, a fun and safe refuge for me from a house of unpredictably timed rages. Joan's parents and brother became for me a model of an emotionally healthy and functional family, despite the fact that her mom struggled with the debilitating effects of metastatic breast cancer that claimed her life at the age of forty-two.

CHAPTER EIGHT

Out of the Manor (Though It Never Really Leaves You)

"The truth shall set you free," Jesus supposedly said. Instead, what he probably said was, "Good luck finding it."

After college, my search for truth led me down many roads, all very far away from the Manor that shaped me into the person I am today, and away from the newly-acquired German-Jewish family that seemed to reject me outright. I thought it was time to "find myself." And in doing so, I ventured far away from the viaducts.

What I know now—but didn't know then—was that I very clearly knew who I was long before I left the Manor to find that person.

My parents saw no choice but to leave the Manor because, by 1970, we were among the few white families left on our block. Many of our neighbors passionately stated they'd prefer to remain in an integrated neighborhood and vowed never to leave. (My mother was the only adult I know who said it and really meant it.) Some of those same neighbors hired moving vans that rumbled down the street after midnight, afraid to admit to those of us who remained that they did not really share a vision of living in an integrated neighborhood.

Many of our parents probably didn't realize that our neighborhood and others north of the viaduct were "redlined," that is, rendered deliberately, legally, and financially off-limits to Blacks. In the Manor and in other redlined Chicago neighborhoods, Blacks were prohibited from seeking FHA government-insured mortgage loans, even in mixed-race neighborhoods. As a result, Blacks were unfairly forced to look at other ways to obtain housing in the 1950s and beyond. One way was to "contract for deed" with white owners. This required a down payment and monthly installments from the new Black occupants to be paid to white landowners. The "sale price" of the house and interest rates could be inflated, and the responsibilities of home ownership were transferred to the new Black inhabitants. The title of the house, however, remained with the white owner, thus creating a category of "slum landlords" (whites that demanded their monthly payments while they retained the home title and had the power to evict Black tenants). These policies very clearly smacked of racism.

My paternal aunt, the infamous Bloody Mary, inherited a portfolio of redlined real estate after her husband died. As a result, she became a very wealthy slumlord in her forties. She drove her huge Buick into Black neighborhoods, extracting pounds of flesh from people who simply wanted to provide decent and affordable homes to their families. It was a role she relished and for which she was well suited.

Here's what I've learned about redlined neighborhoods in Chicago. One study, based on lawsuits, municipal records, and scholarly works, estimated that this predatory "contract for deed" practice from the 1950s to 1970s overcharged Black families between $3.2 and $4 billion dollars (based on 2019 prices) by white real estate agents and slumlords. Later, in the 1970s, the FHA enabled white landlords to sell inner-city properties to Black people at inflated prices, which led to a large number of foreclosures. Clearly, racist policies were set in motion to continue to discriminate against Blacks.

Racism and white privilege were at the very heart of our South Side experience and our exodus from the area. We could afford to leave. And, our parents concluded, we couldn't afford *not* to leave.

But for many in my generation, we didn't comprehend the concepts of racism or white privilege. We were largely insulated from non-whites except on bus rides out of the Manor and into the city. Some of us were victims of what Iram X. Kendi, in his book *How to be An Antiracist*, described as ethnic racism and class racism. We didn't see our white racial privilege. We didn't view ourselves through a racial lens until we were forced to do so (on our trip to Miami Beach in 1962, for example, that I told you about earlier), during the widely televised civil rights demonstrations in Alabama, or after the assassination of Martin Luther King, Jr.

One way of looking at it is that most of the Manor's Jewish youth were born at the intersection of "Never Again" and "White Privilege." Most of us there were born shortly after the end of WWII, after the liberation of barely-breathing human near-skeletons from concentration camps. As we grew up, we learned young that we were born just a few short years after the deliberate and systematic killing of six million Jews and other "undesirables" by Hitler and his gang of sociopaths. As a result, we were made acutely aware of our Jewish identities and the fact that many non-Jews saw us in the crosshairs of their hate-filled biases.

We also later learned that Jew-haters weren't just Nazis but also some of our US ambassadors, the secretary of state, congressmen, and other powerful Americans including Henry Ford and Charles Lindbergh, as well as members of other religious and white ethnic groups who were taught that Jews killed Christ. The Roosevelt administration was fully aware of the atrocities the Nazis were committing and chose to do nothing until the Japanese bombed Pearl Harbor. The Roosevelt administration turned a ship away from a U.S. harbor—the SS *St. Louis*—that was filled to capacity with European Jews trying to enter the U.S. to escape the Nazis. They were not allowed ashore and were sent back to Germany where most perished in concentration camps. It is difficult to grasp that all of this happened less than a decade before we were born.

We were white, but first we were Jewish—some religious and others only culturally. We were different from other white people and we were viewed by non-Jewish whites as being different. In addition to speaking English, we had two other languages—Hebrew and Yiddish.

Yiddish often peppered our English language and was expressed in such ways as:

"Don't be a *schmuck.*" (dual meaning: "jerk" and "penis." Go figure.)
"*Oy vey!*" ("Woe is me!" Also, "Yikes!" or "Wow!")
"You're a pain in the *tuchas* or *tush.* (rear end)
"Kids, will you please stop the *mishagas*? You're giving me a pain in my *kopf.*" (craziness; head)
"Stop being a *kvetch!*" (whiny complainer)
"Stay away from those *goyim.*" (non-Jewish persons)
"You have too many *tchotchkes* to move from Skokie to Arizona." (junky stuff)
"Our *schvartze* high school music teacher was a flaming *fageleh.*" (Black person; homosexual)
"It's so hot and humid outside that I'm *schvitzing.*" (sweating)
"They eat pork chops. Their food is *trayf.*" (non-kosher)
"Let's enjoy a little *nosh.*" (snack)

A pretty girl was a *shaina maidel.* An idiot was a *putz.* A Jew-gone-bad was a *shanda.* At bar and bat mitzvahs, everyone shouted *mazel tov,* a greeting of congratulations. And most of us aspired to be a *mensch,* a decent person.

We had our own religious beliefs. We were not Christian, and we had our own places of worship. Some of us "looked Jewish," with dark hair and enlarged hooked noses that were most often associated with us. (Some of us got nose jobs to both breathe and look better.) We had a certain sensibility that older Jews called *yiddisheh kopfs,* meaning we possessed a distinctively Jewish worldview.

Part of this sensibility led to the prioritization of seeking as much education as possible because, as my Papa told us (and probably every Jewish grandparent did as well), "They can take away your home, take away your possessions, take away your money, but they can't take away your education." He knew this to be true. His family lost everything in Russia. But after immigrating to the U.S. and to Chicago, my Papa and his eight brothers acquired educations and attained comfortable and respectable lives.

We Jews had our own music, our own foods, our own books, our own artifacts (including the aforementioned mezuzahs attached to the doorposts of our homes to proclaim, in Hebrew, our love of God). We had our own Jewish comedians—Shecky Greene, Allen Sherman, Groucho Marx, Woody Allen, George Burns, Jack Benny, and so many others. Some big movie studios were owned by Jews. Many actors and writers were Jewish, although some concealed it. Tragically, many were targeted by Senator Joe McCarthy's Communist blacklisting during the 1940s and 1950s.

Unbeknown to anyone but me, I had a "spiritual experience" at the age of five during a family picnic at Washington Park in Michigan City, Indiana. I quietly wandered away from my family and entered an open arched doorway under a white wooden gazebo. I recall feeling myself falling into a dark, dank, echo chamber. Afraid, I called out to God to save me and suddenly something broke my fall. I concluded: *God saved me!*

I scrambled out of there and hurried back to the family picnic as a BELIEVER. I am still perplexed that, as a frightened five-year-old, I turned to God for help. Why? Because we never, not once, *ever* spoke about God in our home. Neither of my parents were believers, nor were the other Jewish people I knew. I have been a believer since that moment in the gazebo, although I am not an observant Jew. I am what I describe as a cultural Jew. My spiritual experience that day in the gazebo has continued to define me throughout my life.

Being an only child with an emotionally abusive father and an emotionally injured mother left me feeling frightened and vulnerable much of the time. I felt very much alone. There was no one with whom I could share my feelings. I was a shy, quiet kid who increasingly turned to God as my confidante, protector, my entrusted "other." God never left me or disappointed me, even when people did. The problem I encountered, however, was that in the place that I assumed God would be most accessible to a Jewish girl—the synagogue—He/She/It was nowhere to be found.

My Aunt Essie and Uncle Jacob were active members of the Manor's synagogue, a gathering place for many of our neighborhood's

Jewish families. When I was six, I accompanied their daughter (my cousin Jenny who was a year younger than me) to her Sunday school class. When we got there, we encountered pure chaos. There were no adults present to supervise. Kids were yelling and running around the classroom. There were warring factions of little boys in yarmulkes using chalk and erasers from the blackboard as assault weapons. I remember feeling overwhelmed and perplexed. Wasn't this the syn-agogue, the place where God resides? Why does this feel like a crazy place? I was completely turned off to the point that I never returned for a second try. I did, however, continue to accompany my cousins and friends to the children's services, and later to adult services at Congregation Beth Israel (CBI). I never learned to read Hebrew though, and soon felt intimidated by my lack of knowledge. Even though I was a believer, I didn't fit in. My mother was disappointed by my negative experiences at CBI but she never made an attempt to change my mind.

Because my parents weren't at all religious, the temple was of little importance to them. We did occasionally attend Friday night services, but the reality for my parents was that God didn't figure into their life experiences whatsoever. While the synagogue was the Manor's place of Jewish cultural inclusion, I felt an overwhelming sense of disconnection when it became clear to me that God was nowhere to be found there.

What I noticed and experienced at CBI was a pervasive buzzing of people chatting during services, some conversations louder than others. I felt there was a lack of respect for persons who desired to pray, for the rabbi, for the cantor, and for other people. Kids noisily ran in and out of the sanctuary. Preteen girls were frequently huddled together in the women's restroom. Preteen boys were often outside the building while services were being held, with the exception of pre-bar mitzvah boys who were forced to remain in the services.

By the time I was ten years old, I yearned to learn more about Judaism. At my request, my mother approached CBI's rabbi and asked if I could enroll in religious school. He responded that it was too late for me to learn to read Hebrew and added that he suspected my interest was more about wanting to have a bat mitzvah than about wanting to know about Judaism. He was wrong.

Not to be deterred, my mother investigated other synagogues and temples outside of the Manor. We ended up at Sinai Temple in Hyde Park. It was the most reform, liberal temple in all of Chicago, almost completely devoid of Jewish symbols and imagery. What it had going for it was a lack of emphasis on Hebrew and a school bus that picked up children in South Shore and the Manor. And most importantly, Sinai was willing to enroll me in their Sunday school when I was 11.

We referred to the temple as "St. Sinai by the Sea," because of its starkness, lack of traditional Jewish cultural and religious symbols, and its proximity to Lake Michigan. Sinai Temple did not hold regular Shabbat services. Instead, we had Friday night vespers (evening prayer services) in a small chapel and Sunday morning services in the large sanctuary with plush, theater-style seats. We referred to our main rabbi as "Dr. Kraff" rather than Rabbi Kraff.

Even I knew that this felt gentile and radically different from my experiences at the Manor's shul (synagogue). Most of the men at Sinai did not wear a yarmulke. One never saw a tallis (prayer shawl) except on the rabbis and—because they lacked knots on the corners—they more resembled minister's stoles.

A large ark in the sanctuary held Sinai's Torah scrolls. The doors of the ark were controlled by a push-button concealed in the podium on the bima (the raised platform where the Torah is read). The rabbi removed a Torah scroll on Sunday mornings and did a very short Torah reading from a prayer book. All of the prayers were abbreviated and nearly every reading was done responsively in English. There was never a procession with the Torah. A large pipe organ provided the musical background for a professional choir, some of whose members in fact weren't Jewish. The music was beautiful, but it felt more like listening to an operatic performance than liturgical worship. I continued to wonder, *Where is God in this place?*

I was confirmed at Sinai Temple in 1968 when I was sixteen. My parents threw a nice confirmation luncheon in my honor at a hotel in South Shore. My Jewish education was considered complete after my confirmation.

But I persisted. As our son David was preparing for his bar mitzvah in Arizona, I enrolled in the first adult B'nai Mitzvah class at our Arizona conservative synagogue. It was an eighteen-month program, requiring no knowledge of Hebrew, but expanding my insights into Jewish ethics, practices, holidays, and liturgy. It was a good experience. At the end, however, I was still left with an unquenched desire to understand God's place in my daily life. My thirst became a lifelong quest, one that took me well outside of Judaism.

In 1970, my parents moved from the Manor to Skokie to be close to many other diaspora Jews from the South Side. Skokie, Illinois, was as foreign as Nome, Alaska would have been to me. While my parents were settling into their new home, I was fortunate enough to pack my belongings for what was to become four glorious years of undergraduate education in the soybean fields of Urbana-Champaign, Illinois, home of the University of Illinois.

Joan and I were college roommates for three years until Stu and I got married, just before our senior year. For two of those three years, Joan and I shared a small college apartment with two other Southsiders—Darleen and Marilyn—first cousins from Evergreen Park. Almost fifty years later, the four of us are still friends and have enjoyed several roommate reunions over the years. Now, the reality of living far apart, having our own families and grandchildren, dealing with age-related infirmities and other priorities keeps us mostly connected by Facebook and text messages.

Once away from the influence of the Manor and away from my high school and college friends, I dabbled in a variety of healing modalities, few of which offered any therapeutic value whatsoever. I beat back the sharp edges of anxiety with Valium. Estrogen-replacement therapy helped me deal with PMS and post-hysterectomy depression.

My generation is known as "Baby Boomers," but I think it is more accurate to call us "Overdosers." If nothing else, we are a generation of users, infusers, and abusers of most everything. Collectively, we've overdosed on drugs, sex, therapy, education, electronics, email, big-screen TVs, Facebook, Twitter, Instagram, smart phones, tablets, computers, Bluetooth devices, expensive vacations, and our credit cards. Our cars cost far more than the houses we grew up in and are better appointed. Our home stereo systems approach the acoustic integrity of Carnegie Hall. We have acquired more and more in a misguided mission to make us feel good. More RAM. Better acoustics. Better graphics. Better stuff.

Contemplate, meditate, exfoliate. Double lattes have flowed from our pores, espressos through our veins, cold brews through our arteries. Some have solemnly "infused" extra-virgin olive oil with portabellas and porcinis. Our mustards and vinegars are correct, our olives are appropriate for their respective culinary purposes, our herbs are fresh, our vegetables organic. Naturally.

Fitness, you ask? Among my friends, we collectively pursued step aerobics, low-intensity Jazzercise and high-intensity. We religiously tightened abs, tushes, and tits with Mary Magdalene, our personal fitness trainer. Pilates, you ask. Yes, of course. And let's not forget the Pilates Reformer, Zumba, and spinning classes. Hot yoga? Yes, and yoga with a goat on our backs, too.

Later, as a therapist, I explored Freudian psychology, Rogerian, Existential, Ericksonian, Family Systems, Cognitive Behavioral, Mindfulness, and Jungian. I worked on my self-esteem and tried to grow mindful. Namaste.

With the assistance of my spiritual mentor, I tried to deeply cleanse my soul. As a result, I vowed to sacrifice secularism (but not capitalism). With great humility, I moved into the world of the mystics: Kabbalists, the Baal Shem Tov, Isaac Luria, and Caro. To broaden my perspective, I traveled to the vortices of Sedona, Arizona, and the hills of Safed in Israel. I even contemplated relics of St. Anthony in Padua (but his old black tongue and vocal cords just didn't "speak" to my soul).

I traveled thousands of miles from Chicago's South Side, from the bungalows and duplexes and flying milk bottles and chicken-dinnered bar mitzvah parties. Is it any wonder why I chose to leave all that behind? I journeyed from the places I knew best, from paper-thin duplex walls, dank viaducts, and gastronomic Judaism (hold the theology! No God-talk ever!), to find myself.

We all found ourselves in different ways. Stevie Eisner is now known as Steven, lead prosecutor and partner in a mid-sized Chicago law firm. He "found himself" a lot of money and moved to a big house on the North Shore. The only time I see him now is when I'm in Skokie to sit shiva (the weeklong mourning period in Judaism). We're practically strangers now, linked only by fading memories of our imperfect families who lived in side-by-side little boxes with common walls in the Manor. Regardless of the miles and time that now separates us, it is our shared Manor childhoods that keep us from really being strangers.

Stevie's younger sister "found herself" on a national morning television show, telling the story of the suicide of her biracial son. Marla called to tell me to "turn on your TV. You're gonna plotz" (Yiddish for burst). Fortunately, I was still home to see this amazing television moment.

And Ira, a former neighbor down the street, "found himself" behind bars at the state prison in Joliet as a repeat child and wife abuser. Nectarios "found himself" married to Dinky's youngest sister Sophia over at the big Serbian church on Commercial. Nectarios also found Yaya dead a week after his wedding. She was clutching a religious icon, probably because her grandson didn't marry a Greek girl but instead married his very pregnant Serbian girlfriend. His brother Spyridon "found himself" gay and also the co-inheritor of the Mt. Athos Cleaners Extraordinaire along with Nectarios. They eventually moved the business to Wrigleyville, along with Mo Steinberg, Dinky's stylish partner.

CHAPTER NINE

Out of the Manor, Away in the Manger

In my thirties I began the phase of my life that Stu refers to as the "Wonder Years." In search of the God who didn't seem present in any of the synagogues or temples I attended, I ran as far afield from my Jewish upbringing as I could possibly go to "discover my spiritual self." Fortunately, Stu knew me to be a contemplative in college, and somehow loved me in spite of it.

He encouraged me to "be" and he also strongly encouraged me to "stop being" about the time we were both convinced that I was losing my mind. Stu's approach to my intensive spiritual study was that he ignored as much of it as he could for as long as possible until he finally had enough and told me to knock it off. He couldn't understand my devotion to the Benedictine monk who also hailed from the South Side. In hindsight, neither can I.

How did it start?

I worked at a Catholic hospital in Urbana in my mid-twenties. It was there that I experienced a sense of holiness and reverence when attending Catholic masses with my friend, who was a nun. The priests serving mass truly seemed to love Jesus, the liturgy, the sacraments, and those they served. People attending the masses were quiet, polite, and respectful. There was never a drone of competing voices, never an exodus of people during the service. It was serene. It felt sacred.

Since my earlier temple experiences were not in the least bit inspiring or spiritual, shortly after we moved to Arizona, I retreated to the Benedictine House of Prayer in Paradise Valley. It was there that I invoked the M & M's (Merton and meditation), and later, melatonin and martinis in order to get a restful sleep and to retain my youthful looks. I read psalms, lauds, and compline. I chanted. I drummed. Stu only sighs and shakes his head when he thinks back to these "Dark Ages." (Spoiler Alert: I retained my Jewish identity because I had a feeling this wasn't going to last too long. It didn't.)

I joined a select group of suburban contemplatives exploring our spiritual lives in the shadows of Camelback Mountain, in the wealthiest zip code in Arizona. The Spiritual Director's House of Prayer, complete with a built-in Subzero refrigerator/freezer, other high-end appliances, and luxury appointments, sat on a one-plus acre lot alongside a main house with an incredible view of the mountains. It was worth millions of dollars.

"Let us pray," the Spiritual Director intoned, "in the monastic tradition of St. Anthony and the Desert Fathers." (Stu thought they were a heavy metal band in the '60s.). The desert mothers doubtlessly sprayed for scorpions and prepared Jalapeno poppers for a little nosh with their Mogen David while the desert fathers waxed theological.

"We must empty ourselves," chanted the Director. "We must detach fully from our worldly possessions, our vanity, our pride, our egos, our judgments, our expectations." *How about our humanness,* thoughteth me, the graceless sinner in the back of the room, the one in the shadows crawling toward the door? This question wormed its way into my evil little thoughts, worked its way past my treacherous throat, and almost reached my serpentine tongue before being stifled by a stern look from the Spiritual Director. Who can honestly achieve all this and still live in this world? Aspiring mystics want to know.

We listened attentively to the pious and holy words of the Spiritual Director, delicious epithets that dripped liquidly off his tongue in his cozy little house of prayer. At least, until...

I knew in my soul that the Director's words rang a few tones flat.

In a providential encounter, I found him "deeply meditative" while adding a topcoat of Turtle Wax to his new Mercedes convertible. I concluded, admittedly judgmentally, that I should confess that he was not contemplating the spiritual life at all, but rather something far more *this*-worldly.

Perhaps there was something more sacred in his wax job than that which met my corrupted gaze. But more than likely, the voices playing in the Spiritual Director's head were different from the ones I yearned to hear. My voices were becoming mocking and cynical. When I confessed this, the Director told me I was merely an infant in my spiritual maturity, still unable to discern the higher truths.

Faith is a grace given by God, he said, adding that perhaps I am lacking because I have not accepted Jesus Christ as my personal savior. Still, there was something not quite right with his wax job. A new Mercedes convertible, after all, is still a new Mercedes convertible. The only things I appeared to be lacking were blind faith, Turtle Wax, and a clean chamois.

I tried to emulate the disciplined life described by my Spiritual Director. But deep in my soul I queried, "Is this really what God wants of me, oh Creator of Lexuses, Contemplator of Audis, Curator of Range Rovers? Domini, Domini, Domini...roger and out." In praying for the holy gifts of grace, mercy, and humility, few confess it is the acquisition of stuff that occupies most of our thoughts, including those of the Spiritual Director.

He was a charmer, to be sure, a beckoning seducer and dangler of words filled with promises of deliverance and salvation from the emptiness of the corporeal landscape. Sweet words about how to become more holy...like him. I couldn't stifle the thought that something wasn't kosher here!

According to the Christian Bible, Jesus instructed his apostles to "remember me" after he died. If so, did Jesus *really* expect his followers to remember him by eating his flesh and drinking his blood? (I imagined the ring on my finger: WWVD? What would vegetarians do?) Is this what Jesus *really* wanted believers to do? And, if so, why is it that *only* priests can trans-substantiate bread and wine into the *actual* body and blood of Christ? What kind of magical powers do priests receive in seminaries? Are they some sort of wizards?"

I concluded that it really didn't sound like anything I could ever possibly believe.

(NOTE: Of course, I learned that many Protestants do not believe they are *literally* consuming Christ's body and blood when they "remember Jesus" as they receive communion. But some Protestants do, along with Catholics and Eastern Orthodox Christians.)

I didn't have any issues with the *man* Jesus, the poor Jewish rabbi from Bethlehem and Nazareth who purportedly spent his early adult life preaching love, acceptance, and forgiveness, and advocating for the poorest and most vulnerable people.

I did, however, have an issue with artists whose masterpieces depicted blond-haired, blue-eyed, Aryan-looking Jesuses who clearly were not of Middle Eastern origin. Were these Jesuses from Dusseldorf? Amsterdam? Copenhagen? Exactly what artistic and political statements were these artists making? Did the religious powers-that-be require artists to paint white, blond, blue-eyed Jesuses to depict white supremacy?

Overall, my primary issues were with powerful men both pre- and post-crucifixion: those who politicized and interpreted the words of Jesus, those who determined what writings would (and would not) be included in the Christian canon, those who created and perpetuated a distilled narrative including "actual" quotes of Jesus (appearing in red type in some Christian Bibles, as if anyone remembered *exactly* what Jesus said when oral narratives were written down much later).

Indeed, it was powerful men who created religions and sects to worship Jesus and Mary with exclusionary and strange beliefs, rituals, and sacraments that in essence said, "If you don't believe and practice *exactly* the way we do, your beliefs and practices are wrong." And it was powerful men who depicted Mary Magdalene as a whore. (Although some theological scholars believe she was Jesus' wife.)

Why *should* Jesus die for our sins? I mean, why would God sacrifice his beloved son to save us if, as advertised, remorse, repentance, and a radical change from sinful behaviors weren't prerequisites for our salvation? Shouldn't it be *our* responsibility to become better people and to learn from our mistakes? To make amends with those we've offended or harmed? To make amends with God?

And what about confessing one's sins? How does the repetition of 20 Hail Marys compensate for the sin of stealing from the local farmer's fields? Or sexually abusing children? Or lying to Congress or the American people? Or using one's white supremacy to randomly murder persons of color? The repetition of Hail Marys doesn't seem to have much influence in motivating a sinner to stop sinning, as far as I'm concerned.

After further study and much discernment, I concluded that I didn't believe Jesus was born to a virgin impregnated by God or that Jesus overcame death on a cross, or that faith in Jesus through baptism was all that was required in order to be expunged of one's sins with the "bonus guarantee" of everlasting life.

And why does it matter if Jesus was or wasn't married? Why can't priests marry in the Catholic Church but are allowed to marry in other Christian denominations? Does marriage really detract from one's devotion to serving God? And why, *for heaven's sake*, can't women become priests when they can be ordained as pastors in other Christian denominations?

And this: Why is baptism a guarantee for eternal life when, in some Christian denominations, babies are baptized without *any* awareness or understanding of the meaning of the sacrament? The concept of a newborn baby having "Original Sin" didn't make sense. The story of Adam and Eve told how, as adults, they didn't follow God's explicit command to stay away from the Tree of Knowledge. Instead, they plucked and ate fruit from the tree. As a result of their defiance, God punished them and all of their offspring. But why would *anyone* infer from this story that every newborn infant is stamped with Original Sin from the moment they exit the womb (with the only antidote being baptism)? Newborn babies are pure and innocent. How can they sin from the moment they are born?

And why do so many baptized Christians believe that those Jews who fervently worship one God will go to hell because we haven't accepted Jesus as our personal savior? After all, Jesus was born a Jew, and he died a Jew. He was a radical, observant Jew preaching ideas that threatened powerful Jewish priests and Romans. He was outspoken. He challenged the status quo. But he was a Jew, *not* a Christian, throughout his entire life.

After much introspection, I concluded that Jesus was a pious Jewish man with courage and grace, a man who embodied virtuous traits. He apparently was a loving and accepting man of faith and goodness, a radical thinker. For these reasons, Jesus was worth remembering and emulating. At the same time, however, I also concluded that Jesus was not God incarnate any more than is any other human being.

And then I began to meditate upon the very essence of God. Over time, I came to believe that God is a "Higher Power" of indeterminate magnitude, traits, and abilities, a non-corporeal, amorphous otherness with mostly unknown attributes. We use the name "God" for lack of a better word to describe this ethereal force.

Why do we refer to God as a He or a She? This implies male or female personhood. Not once have I doubted my belief in a "Higher Power," but rather in the ways we attribute human qualities and traits to God, and in the ways we presume knowledge of a Higher Power that transcends human understanding. Do I feel a personal connection to this Higher Power? Yes. But I never attempt to understand the connection or describe it. It simply is.

After all my reflections, I concluded that religious symbols and rituals are incorporated into religious practices for the purpose of stoking and evoking emotions. Ever since humans conceived of God, powerful men have created narratives, beliefs, practices, and exclusionary rules to impose on ordinary men and women. It is the very nature of humans to exert power and control over less powerful people. It isn't a Christian thing or a Jewish thing. Sadly, it is a *human* thing.

Meanwhile, back at the House of Prayer...

The Director regularly reminded me that basically I am less worthy than pond scum. This, he said, is good for my soul, adding something akin to "the first come last, and the last come first."

His approach had me wondering: Does God listen when we tell Him/Her/It exactly what we want? Are our prayers better and more pleasing to God after we make a hefty donation to the House of Prayer Stewardship fund? Holy books lined the Spiritual Director's shelves like trophies on a mantle. What game has he won? Neither of us has risen yet. As far as I could see, we're both at the same starting gate.

Who knows what comes first and what comes next? Sweet holy mysteries beckon us while narcissistic clergy persons of all faiths, cultists, and Pied Piper gurus crush our spirits and smother our souls with their versions of "truth." Incongruities abound and confuse us. Spinners of truth twist us into fools with their manipulations. How did things get so crazy?

After all of this tumult and questioning, I remained both a cultural Jew and a believer in a Higher Power. I appreciated some of the contributions and wisdom gleaned from Judaism as well as from other diverse belief systems. I still do. What I mainly learned on my personal journey is that we are all just infants in our spiritual lives no matter our ages, and that includes the Spiritual Director who was last seen hitchhiking on the road to salvation after his Mercedes convertible got a flat.

CHAPTER TEN

God, the Dog, and the Teenager

More than twenty years ago, I sat on the edge of a hideaway sofa bed listening to the sounds of someone else's family—a cacophony of hairdryer noises humming, teenage phone conversations, discourses with the family dog about the necessity of pooping outside in spite of a driving rain, and more. These are typical sounds of families from one coast to the next. Phones ringing, voices with too much emotion and not enough content. Conversations filled to brimming about the next dinner, the last get-together, the next dance recital. I listened and observed. I found these sounds surprisingly pleasing.

Glancing out the window, my tired eyes witnessed family tapestries woven with fibers of love, of accommodation, of compromise, of hope, and of mild-to-acute anxiety. As I sat there, I began to feel like some twisted old thread in a bent and long-forgotten needle, back again to be rewoven into a corner of this garment of life. I saw how reality continually challenges us to sacrifice, repent, forgive... and then to let go and move on.

I was taken with their dog, a flop-eared little dust mop who keeps his end of the conversation simply by raising an obstinate ear and stiffening his body as if to say, "I shall poop when I am good and ready." Simple. Not a complex thought. No need for multi-syllabic words. No grandiosity, religiosity, politics, or innuendo. The simple gesture of a well-exercised ear muscle speaks volumes and lets everyone know who truly is in charge. At six pounds, this little fluff of doggy dander ruled his domain. Nobody was foolish enough to dispute this fact.

Next in command was the teenager of the family, given to grand performances of pouty moods and drama of epic proportions. As an outsider to this one-act play, I observed this sixteen-year-old masterful storyteller write the script and perform as leading lady, director, and producer on this living stage of suburban life. (I hadn't realized that this next generation had evolved with Velcro ears, an adaptive mutation necessary to hold a cell phone firmly in place at all times.)

What I experienced here, in fact, is a universal truth. In addition to spiritual gurus and mass marketers, dogs and teens rule the earth, keep us trained well, and always connected to *their* leads.

It was no different in my home. The bark changes, but the bite is the same (be it from a dog or a teenager).

The reality is that our children are always in the process of leaving us, moment by moment, preparing to hear new sounds in new places with new people and new voices. As parents of teenagers, it seems we're no longer truly wanted (although our credit cards are truly needed). This comes as no great insight but certainly as a shock. After all, everyone is always leaving, always moving on, and sooner or later always coming back to find that place from which to leave again. One is here and gone, wanting to be held, but resisting the hold that is too tight, too confining.

We continually try to master some dance, but we don't quite know the steps, can't hear the music, can't feel the beat. We strain to feel the music, but it eludes us. Our children are no different. Too soon it is almost time for them to leave us, to dance their own dances. We know it and we suffer. They know it and they also know we must suffer. So, they help us suffer with a little too much enthusiasm.

The dog decided I was family now, anointing my nose with random and welcoming licks and baptizing the sheets of the sofa bed with doggy spit. I passed the sniff test and became well acquainted with the dog, a medium to help us humans bridge the gaps of time and distance and intimate connectedness now strained by too many silences and lapses of caring. I am on the road again, home for now from the spirit world, back to the bittersweet smells of suburban humanity. It sure feels good...well, sort of.

In a moment of exhilaration while caught up in the passions of atonement—as is the fashion of many Jewesses late in the summertime—I contacted Joan, my best friend from Bowen High School Class of 1970 and my college roommate for three years. Mountain Airlines was running a fantastic can't-miss promotion. "Whadya think about a reunion?" I queried.

"Cool," she responded, with a hint of enthusiasm and another of hesitation, the latter which I should have zeroed in on but instead ignored.

So, I flew out to see her. Where does one begin after the hellos are spoken, the double chins are counted, the new hair colors are admired, the wrinkles are duly noted? Amazingly, she passed me at Barnes & Noble within hours of my arrival, having forgotten what I now look like! Have I changed that much? I guess it must be the chin line, the crow's feet, and the waistline.

Amazingly, two score and fifteen years ago, we shared a dorm room the size of a bathroom scale, which concealed nothing and revealed every inch of our budding adult bodies. But we remained linked by common memories, shared religious experiences, and our love for our husbands, our kids, and our dogs. We (re)discovered that we both like to shop, go to movies and to eat. A lot.

But panic and social anxiety still bubbled up inside of me as I realized we were both captives of the same airline promotion. I intruded into their home, disturbed their structured patterns, and added complexity. Before long, we were left groping for words and devices with which to build new bridges and to revive our fading memories of the times we shared.

"Remember," I asked, "when we were freshmen in college and we read about orgasms in *Cosmo* and we didn't know how to pronounce it, let alone what it meant?" She didn't remember.

"Remember," she asked, "when I thought my house was on fire and my mother was at the grocery store, so you rode your bike through the Paxton viaduct and went all the way up to 87th Street to find my mom at the grocery store?" I remembered. It took me an hour to catch my breath after that bike ride.

Unfortunately, some of our memories had faded and our brain-spaces were now filled with more recent, unshared memories.

Thank goodness for the dog and teenager! How they filled awkward silences!

While playing with her dog, each of us confessed that we converse more easily with our respective dogs than with our respective teenaged children. This fact comforted us and fueled the synapses for a new connection: an existential loneliness that we each confessed as we shared our attempts to mother our teenaged children and routinely found their bedroom doors—and their private thoughts—closed to us.

Shopping malls and movies remained a favorite pastime for both of us and served as a perfect escape from the unspoken awareness we shared in knowing that our lives now fly in fully separate orbits. We were no longer intersected, no longer vital to one another. At the same time, we knew we maintained a pleasurable and permanent bond that connected our hearts, even though we no longer knew the other's fetishes, friends, or foes.

Many of our same old, annoying habits remained as relics. It was amazing how readily we fell into our same ancient patterns. She still found me to be an insufferable know-it-all. I found that we still do what she wants to do when she wants to do it and that I still give in (and still sometimes resent it afterward.) She still takes well over an hour to get dressed in the morning, and I still wait and wait for her to get done. Some things never change. And everything changes except this: You are a South Sider, no matter where you live, unless you choose to deny who you really are. Only one person I've ever known actually did that, and I'll tell you about him in a little while.

CHAPTER ELEVEN

Our Genealogies

You never stop being a South Sider unless you choose to, even when you move 1,738 miles away and end up living quite by accident in the Twelve Oaks Ward of the Church of Jesus Christ of Latter-day Saints in Tempe, Arizona. That's what the two tall blond boys with their short-sleeved white shirts, black pants, black bicycles, and black-and-white name tags told me the first time anybody rang our doorbell at our new home. They even gave us as a housewarming gift: our very own copy of *The Book of Mormon*.

Actually, when that happens, you realize you just can't stop yourself from being a South Sider because otherwise you wouldn't recognize yourself at all. There are only a few things even close to the South Side around here, like the dry cleaners and shoe repair shops, both of which still smell pretty much the same as the ones on 95th Street. We also have a restaurant nearby called House of Lychee, which absolutely amazed my mother and me.

Mother and her neighbor friend Bertha Eisner used to pull their grocery carts over to The Lychee Hut on 95th Street, order egg foo young, light up Salems, and pull a few bugs from their food each time, even though the owners insisted they weren't bugs, but rather "lychees with legs," whatever those are. Bertha liked the egg foo young so much that she was able to make that leap of faith and seemed content to remove *lychees* (those slippery little Oriental vegetables) one by one. Mother went along with the program, too, although I noticed that she started ordering chicken chow mein instead, and she politely asked the owners to "Please hold the lychees as I seem to be allergic to them." It's no wonder I stopped eating there. Fortunately, our Arizona House of Lychee has not offered up those little things with arms and legs that used to wave at us.

The other thing that feels like the South Side is our temple, Congregation Beth Am of Arizona. As I mentioned earlier, back home in the Manor, many neighborhood Jews worshipped at Congregation Beth Israel. CBI's spiritual leader was a middle-aged gentleman with a strange affect. Many Jews in our neighborhood went to CBI, even a few goyim including Spyridon, Nectarios' brother, who mostly got hauled to the Greek Orthodox Church on Stony Island. Only the Catholics didn't come to CBI because Marla's sister Jackie said they ate flesh and drank blood across the street at the Holy Heart of Mary Roman Catholic Church and Bingo Hall.

Father McAfee told Billy, our next-door neighbor to the north, and the other Catholics at mass one Sunday that the Jews had killed Jesus. Billy later told me that, because he thought the priest meant that it was my family that had crucified Jesus, he baptized me later that Sunday with my father's garden hose. He did it, he said, because he liked me.

CBI was housed in a building pieced together with Double Bubble bubblegum, plywood, and chicken wire where the sanctuary was adjoined to the Hebrew School. The grownups couldn't understand why the whole building smelled like old chewing gum and urinal cakes. Fortunately, of the two aromas, the most pervasive was unmistakably that of vintage Double Bubble.

At night, when the wind rattled the windows really hard, you just knew that stormtroopers were probably going to break in with Father McAfee as the chief commando. Actually, we did catch a real, live neo-Nazi at CBI one Friday night in 1969.

My cousin Jenny and I were up on the bima singing a duet of "Sim Shalom" at the BBG Teen Service. Just as we were returning to our seats, a brick smashed through one of the windows, narrowly missing a college chemistry professor who lived in our neighborhood. Several of my neighbors, along with my father, rushed out in the middle of Shabbat service. The rabbi was visibly shaken, but somehow managed to continue the service.

About forty minutes later, our CBI militia, with my father at the fore, hauled a pimply-faced fellow up to the bima. I'll never forget the mixture of anger and fear in the sanctuary that night. For the first time ever at CBI, you could hear a pin drop as the Nazi wannabe apologized, tears streaming down his face. My father, I learned later, was twisting his arm very, very hard. The rabbi apparently was the only one besides my father who actually heard the kid's arm pop out of its socket. For the first time ever, the rabbi spoke kindly to my father.

After that night, my dad was asked to be the CBI greeter, which effectively made him the temple's "bouncer." It is especially noteworthy that we were not members of CBI. However, this was a job for which my father was well suited and that he gladly accepted. Since he was not a religious man, my father slept very soundly through the services but he always made a remarkable recovery in time to enjoy Bubbie's challah and cookies during the oneg, the social gathering that typically followed the service.

CBI's rabbi was nothing like our Arizona rabbi, an articulate female feminist from Brooklyn. Temple Beth Am's building in Arizona, however, is very similar to CBI's, except in some respects our Arizona shul is even worse. Mormons sold it to us after they were firmly convinced they wouldn't set foot in it again as it was in such a state of disrepair. They petitioned the powers that be for a new building and got one.

We, the 170 affiliated conservative Jewish families in the area, weren't as fortunate in that our funds were quite limited. Unlike our Mormon neighbors who faithfully tithe a hefty 10 percent of their incomes, Jewish pioneers have a hard time committing their dollars to our faith communities. So, we do the next best thing: we complain incessantly about the peeling paint, toilets that don't flush, and air conditioning that often breaks down in the middle of summer. Instead, we dedicate our dollars to throwing lavish bar mitzvah parties at five-star resorts, with deejays and belly dancers.

One memorable Arizona Sabbath at Temple Beth Am brought a chance meeting with a former Manorite. Jack Cohen, Bowen class of 1969, moved with his family to Arizona shortly after we did. He grew up near Richard Speck's "Shop of Horrors" just down the street from our grade school. Later, as the Manor became integrated, his family moved up to the predominantly white North Side, where people lived in single-family homes and where its citizens didn't have the same problem as Southsiders when pronouncing "th" sounds in words such as the, that, than, them, those, and this. I noticed that Jack's diphthongs were remarkably well articulated, while mine in contrast still reflect the distinctive "duh" Manor idiolect that makes us sound like real idiots.

When Blacks eventually outnumbered whites in the Manor, many of the remaining families panicked and moved quickly, largely due to the careful prodding of "block-busters," the predatory realtors responsible for the Manor's transformation. My parents moved north, too, along with my aunt and her family. After CBI was sold to the Faith and Truth A.M.E. Church of Holiness in Christ, the rabbi and his wife moved up north too.

The only difference between my family's move to Skokie and that of Jack's family was that my family never stopped identifying as being Southsiders. My parents were "diaspora" Southsiders, exiled to Skokie as a result of my father's perception of sheer necessity. Jack's family, in contrast, gladly renounced "those South Side ways" the moment they moved up north. And that's what they called it—*moving up*.

Jack happily cashed in his South Side soul for something he thought was far better but which, in fact, turned out to be utterly and remarkably ordinary. He married Susie, a real suburban North Sider who, rather predictably, had about as much in common with Southsiders as I do with the Mormon missionaries who are ringing my doorbell as I write this.

My disappointment came not with the revelation that Susie and I shared few common values. Rather, it was the awareness that her husband was an apostate who eagerly renounced his Manor origins.

That was due in no small part to the fact that Susie could in no way identify with his incredibly rich, and paradoxically simple, beginnings. Nor did she care to acknowledge that her children came from a geographically compromised gene pool. Susie aspired to a better way of life and it didn't take Albert Einstein to sniff out a social climber of epic proportions.

Unfortunately for Jack and Susie, their income did not come close to those who live in Scottsdale's Jewish neighborhoods. So, they did the next best thing and bought someone else's used "real custom home" in a real custom goyish neighborhood. (This, my husband said, would be equivalent to an Orthodox Jew buying a custom home in Berwyn or Cicero.) Perhaps others are impressed. We are simply disappointed when we experience a South Sider-gone-bad.

I was talking to Katherine, a Mormon friend, the other day about our respective genealogies. She can trace her ancestry back for six generations. Her great-great-grandparents were Mormon pioneers who moved across the country to homestead near the Great Salt Lake. Her great-great-Uncle Jebediah was martyred in Nauvoo, Illinois.

When Katherine asked me about my genealogy, I groaned. My grandparents on my mother's side were born somewhere in Russia but were forced to flee in the late 1890s because of anti-Semitic Cossacks who pillaged their villages. We have no idea in what towns they lived or the names of their grandparents. My familial ties were to my mother's sister Essie who lived with her family just down the street from us in the Manor. We spent a lot of time with them. My dad's parents died long before I was born and, since he hated his oldest sister, I never really knew most of his family.

Many of my husband's extended family died in German concentration camps, although the lucky ones (including his grandparents and parents) miraculously got out in time.

I told Katherine that my "family" was mostly the extended-type and included the Maslows, Glicksteins, Adamskys, Appelowitzes, Brownsteins, Lerners, Eisners, Greenbergs, Kronenfelds, and Sack-houses, all from the South Side. My family tree was firmly rooted there by way of Russia, Poland, Lithuania, and Ellis Island, and we eventually homesteaded just south of Pill Hill on the other side of the viaduct. A small seedling of that family tree blew in the wind to Skokie. Thirty years later, another seed somehow landed in Arizona.

CHAPTER TWELVE

It is the Rare Episcopalian Who Plays Mahjong

The move from the Midwest to Arizona was difficult for me and almost impossible for my parents. In the tradition of Jewish parents, they hid from me the fact that my father had been diagnosed with a terminal illness because, although I was thirty-seven, they didn't want "to be a burden."

So, they chose instead to thoroughly shock me on the day Mother could no longer find the energy to clean his fifth soiled bedsheet of the morning. My mother later told me that she fell to the floor in exhaustion, wrapped in that stinky, soiled sheet. I knew he hadn't been feeling well, but I had no idea until I got that call that he was slowly dying—and that my mother's diabetes was advancing.

I made five separate trips to Chicago that summer. My first trip was intended to "assess the situation." Within thirty minutes of my arrival, I started to clean out papers that dated back to the time of my parents' engagement.

In what the family referred to as "Debbie's room" (strangely named since I never really lived in it and they turned it into a study), I found my old prom dress, grade school autograph book, high school scrapbooks, and forty-six never-used matchbooks from my confirmation party in 1968.

While I inventoried a lifetime of my family's stuff, my husband kept busy preparing himself and our then-eight-year-old son David for the reality that our lives were about to change. Stu signed a lease on a 600-square-foot, two-bedroom apartment in a senior apartment building near our home in Tempe, Arizona. He moved furniture that we purchased for my parents into this alien place far, far away from the Manor or anything remotely resembling Chicago.

Meanwhile, in Chicago, I soon learned that my mother steadfastly held onto *every* receipt, bank statement, and tax return that ever crossed her palm, "in case we get audited." I said it was unlikely they'd be audited in 1989 for a stove purchased in 1953, but she said, "You just never know, and who's it hurting anyway?" "Me," I cried, four hours into Trip #1, at the moment Mother and I were excavating the bowels of the fifty-two giant family-sized garbage bags stuffed with personal records.

Marla, my first friend in the world, thought I was having a nervous breakdown. (Truth be told, I think I was!) To keep me from killing myself or my mother, Marla filled me full of dirt, stories about the Pincus' son, and about assorted perverts from the old neighborhood. She also stuffed me full of Lou Malnati's Pizza, a true Chicago antidote to insanity.

By my second trip to Chicago that spring, an angel by the name of Patrick Shanahan came into our lives. For no apparent reason, he fell in love with my parents' little, nondescript Skokie house. In fact, he paid a premium price to my parents, according to my real estate attorney cousin. While we were busy knocking on everything wood for our incredible and unexpected luck, Patrick stunned us one more time by offering to purchase my parents' furniture, every last piece of God-awful orange and green velour-striped stuff. What was wrong with him? Was he blind?

To this day, I believe Patrick Shanahan was an angel of God, Holy Redeemer of the Southsiders in Exile in Skokie. Over the course of his home purchase and beyond, Patrick became a true friend of my mom's. In fact, a year after purchasing their house, he sent a package to her in Arizona that contained the flap from the old metal mailbox that he'd replaced with a new mailbox. It was a souvenir from their Skokie days.

Each of our subsequent visits to Skokie before my mom's death included a visit with Patrick. He showed us the new additions to his home, including a garage, hardwood floors, granite countertops, new appliances, and my parents' velvet furniture moved downstairs into an "apartment" he created for his godson and his wife.

But I digress.

My most formidable challenges lay ahead in Trips #3 and #4 during which I tried to separate my father from the basement full of his "collectibles," dubious treasures that he hoarded in the basement, including things he'd bought and things I'm fairly certain he'd stolen.

I attempted a calm and rational appeal: "You're moving from a 1,200-square-foot home to a 600-square-foot apartment. Something's got to go, Dad."

"Not my hula girl," he bellowed. "Keep your hands off my stuff!"

My father held tough and questioned every move I made. *Every* move. Together, Marla and I resigned ourselves to making neat piles labeled: "Move to Arizona," "Jewish charities," and "Only Mrs. Pincus deserves this pile of shit."

It was the "Pincus Pile" that caused the biggest wars between my father and me because it was in the Pincus pile that my father's favorite plastic flowers-that-didn't-look-like-flowers-at-all ended up. Along with old statues that he'd probably found in someone else's garbage cans, broken and empty picture frames, dozens of rusty nails, and thirty-nine cans of dried-up Sherwin-Williams paint with the dates 1956, 1962, and 1967 scribbled on their lids. My father argued that Stu would find a use for them in Arizona. My fingers clenched involuntarily. I was almost catatonic.

By this point in my father's illness, he mainly slumped over his cane for support. The only time I saw him walk erect that summer was to move from the back door to the alley to remove our Pincus Pile from the dumpster and to return his treasures to his beloved paneled basement. This was a man with a mission, totally at cross-purposes with my own.

Meanwhile, the Pincus Pile quickly grew to the size of a small Arizona foothill. When I told my parent's next-door neighbors about the utter futility of moving my father's treasures to their ultimate junkyard destination, Mrs. Cohen truly felt sorry for me. So sorry, in fact, that she cleared out her aluminum shed and allowed me to hide the Pincus Pile inside, serving as a "way station" to their personal garbage cans which Mr. Cohen filled each evening. Without the cunning help of the Cohens, my parents never would have moved to Arizona.

Another memorable moment on that trip occurred when it was time to whittle down my father's huge collection of indoor and outdoor tools. He did not want to part with his hammers, screwdrivers, and other hardware items. "Fine," I said, "take them."

But when it came to his snowblower, snow shovels, and six-foot aluminum ladder, I thought he would blow a gasket. "Please," I implored my cousin Kenny, "don't you have a need for this wonderful snowblower and snow shovels? And for this sturdy metal ladder?" Kenny acknowledged they would all come in handy. None of these implements were new or in the greatest condition, but they still worked.

My father bellowed, "If you want them, what are you going to pay me for them?"

"Dad," I begged, "Kenny can use them and you're not going to need them in Tempe, Arizona. Let's give them to him."

After much grousing, my father grudgingly agreed and reminded Kenny that, due to his beneficence, he was getting some "good deals." My cousin Jenny agreed to take our Nonny and Papa's heavily carved mahogany furniture from my parents' basement. My father knew better than to try to negotiate a sale price for furniture that was never his.

Eventually, thanks to the Cohens, Marla, and my incredible cousins, the overwhelming pile of a lifetime's memories was eventually whittled into something almost manageable. The final trip actually went without a hitch, once we made it through the real estate closing. There were also the long-anticipated farewell breakfasts, luncheons, and dinners, and the showers of tears that came with the final slamming of the door of the much-hated Skokie house. Irv, my parents' lifelong friend, stood on the sidewalk and sobbed as my mother gripped the doorknob and pulled it shut.

About two weeks after Stu carried my mother over their new Arizona threshold, she phoned and asked, "Do you think Episcopalian women play Mahjong?" This was a subject that never, not even once, crossed my mind. I was, in fact, utterly stunned by the question.

"Uh, well, um...why would you ask such a thing?" I stammered stupidly.

"The Episcopal Women's Circle from St. Stephen's meets in our card room on Thursday afternoons. My neighbor Edith is in the circle and she asked if I'd like to attend the next meeting with her. She said some of the newer ladies don't play cards. Do you think they play Mahjong?"

It turned out they didn't, but after two weeks of lessons led by my mother, her little addiction was soon shared with a few of the newer members of the Episcopal Women's Circle. They also learned an important truth about Jewish women: you can move a Jewish lady almost anywhere, but you can't take her Mahjong tiles away. Mother became the first Jewish member of the St. Stephen's Episcopal Women's Circle. By Passover, she had them eating matzo with Cheez Whiz.

Chapter Thirteen

Chex Mix, Lipton Onion Soup Dip and Cheese Whiz: The Essential Manor Food Groups

There are certain sounds, sights, smells, and tastes that, for me, are so much a part of the Manor that it's impossible to think about experiencing them anywhere else. But much to my amazement, not only did my parents move to Tempe, Arizona, so did certain South Side cultural artifacts.

My mother was the only Jewish lady on earth capable of transforming the ladies of St. Stephen's Episcopal Church in Tempe to dedicated Mahjong mavens in the space of two months. Father Bruce, senior rector of St. Stephen's, was so smitten with my mother that he gave the homily at my father's Arizona memorial service, while our own rabbi played a much smaller role.

Along with Mahjong Mother "baptized" the Episcopal ladies with the rich, artery-clogging, gallbladder-meltdown dubbed by Marla as "the Manor Mahjong Food Group." Every South Sider knew this consisted of a well-laid spread that featured Lipton Onion Dip with REAL sour cream, rippled Jay's Potato Chips, Mr. Peanut-brand salted peanuts, and Cheez Whiz with Ritz Crackers.

Actually, Cheez Whiz in any form was acceptable. For example,

Erma once brought a delicious little Cheez Whiz and Smoked Salmon Mousse with sesame crackers. She blended it with Philadelphia brand cream cheese and shredded pineapple "to give it a subtle yet tangy flavor."

Once—and only once—did Mother go a little haywire and buy pimento cheese in spray cans to serve to her friends in the Manor. Bertha somehow lost her grip on the nozzle and ended up spraying cheese all over our new sofa. Fortunately for Bertha, Mother kept stiff plastic covers on every piece of furniture we owned so the pimento cheese wiped up easily with a damp sponge. Unfortunately for those of us who wore shorts in the summer, however, and sat on those plastic-covered sofas, our thighs became painfully fused to the plastic. (We were sure extensive skin grafts would be required.)

Chex Mix was eventually included because Mrs. Pincus insisted it was "the rage" on the North Side. My father quite enjoyed this newfangled amalgam of cereals. He enjoyed it so much, in fact, that he invested their small nest egg in General Foods. It turned out to be a pretty good investment.

These foods—and generally no others—were served at countless Mahjong games in the living room of our Manor duplex. A mixture of smell from the cigarettes, Cheez Whiz, and onion dip wafted up the staircase into my room, even with my door closed. The sounds were equally memorable: the clicking of the Mahjong tiles, cackling Mahjong mavens and screeching sounds of their laughter at decibels that would shatter a wine glass. These were mighty Manor Jewish women doing what they did best. (Jenny still swears that my mom always smelled like Cheez Whiz.)

It is the rare Episcopalian who plays Mahjong. But somehow my mother worked her magic and before long, a whole roomful of Arizona Episcopalian Mahjong players emerged, much to her delight.

As a recent transplant to Arizona, she soon made new friends of these proper Episcopalian ladies. Not a gregarious bunch in that they effused little emotion it was still quite apparent that they loved my mother.

Stu thinks they loved her because of her sweetness and genuine lack of pretense. I agree with that. But I also think they admired her creative Cheez Whiz creations. By the way, here's a favorite recipe of hers from the Manor B'nai B'rith Cookbook. This particular recipe was created by Gertie Leventhalinskywitz. Her "Cheezy Chow Bowl" won first place in the B'nai B'rith Cook-off in 1965.

GERTIE'S CHEESY CHOW BOWL

Ingredients:

6 oz. Cheez Whiz or melted cheese food (Velveeta, etc.) at room temperature

3 oz. of Corn Chex or Purina Puppy Chow "for a toothsome crunch" (just kidding about the Puppy Chow!)

1 small jar of pimentos

1 small can of creamed corn

1 12-oz. can of crushed pineapple (reserve the heavy syrup to reconstitute the Puppy Chow)

1 tin of anchovies or sardines in oil

A sprinkle of paprika for "pazazz" and some dried parsley for "garnush"

With a mallet, pound Corn Chex or Puppy Chow into a coarse "crumb-like" consistency. Mix all ingredients well and shape in a ball. Enjoy with Cheez Doodles or Ritz crackers.

My father always managed to sneak some of the Mahjong snacks that my mom prepared for her friends before they arrived. When the Arizona ladies came over to play, my father would take a walk "to get a little fresh air." My mom was happy that my dad was doing something healthy. What she didn't know, however, was that my diabetic father was walking to the nearby donut shop, Winchell's (prophetically perhaps, the "Winc" neon letters on the sign were burned out), to enjoy a few sweet delectables. Other times, he would head out to the nearby Thrifty's to inhale a double scoop of chocolate ice cream. He never confessed where his walks took him, and my mother never asked. She was simply content that he enjoyed his walks in the neighborhood *and* that he made himself scarce while she was entertaining her friends. (When Stu and I confronted him about these "health" walks, he begged us not to tell my mother. We respected his wishes.)

My father's world in Arizona became very small as his health deteriorated. We sold his car in Skokie before they moved to Tempe because he could no longer drive. He could no longer enjoy gardening either, although the landscape crew at the senior complex allowed my father the opportunity to water the bushes on their spacious grounds. After a while, my father became weaker and was unable to do even that.

My father and a retired Lutheran minister—Pastor Bill who also lived in the complex—became close friends and often traded jokes and stories about WWII. The second bedroom in my parents' apartment was set up as my father's hobby and nap room, complete with a small desk, bookshelves for his stamp collection, and a twin trundle bed for his naps. Over time, he started sleeping longer and longer hours as the toxins in his body overwhelmed his liver and kidneys.

CHAPTER FOURTEEN

Better Hide the Matches, the Waitress is Coming

There were no decent restaurants south of the viaduct, particularly the kind one would choose for a dress-up family dinner. Once a year, we got all dolled up because our North Side relatives were invited to make their annual pilgrimage into the low rent district. It is particularly noteworthy that they never visited our duplex or Aunt Essie's. I think they were embarrassed for us or maybe for themselves.

When I was twelve, I suggested that we rent out Moishe's Pippic, the hot dog joint near Benny's kosher butcher shop. I figured we could all play the pinball machines and listen to the jukebox while the older relatives visited.

My mother and Aunt Essie opted instead to host these special events twelve miles away in Whiting, Indiana, at Vittle's Restaurant and Banquet Hall, just down Indianapolis Boulevard from the Lever Brothers factory and Phil Smidt's famous perch and frog leg palace.

My cousin Jenny and I so hated these family dinners that we always planned a caper to help pass the time. One year, Jenny suggested we pull the fire alarm to see what would happen, but I wasn't willing to go that far. Being the older cousin, I concluded we'd run the risk of doing some major damage and I didn't think that was such a good idea. (I also knew how my father would react, and it would not have been good.)

Instead, Jenny got some matches to ignite a roll of toilet paper in the ladies' room. I agreed this sounded like fun. Jenny wanted to set the roll on fire while it was still on the spindle attached to the stall. I, the more conservative cousin, insisted that we exercise "good judgment" and at the very least not ignite it until it was near a water source. The toilet, for whatever reason, didn't count.

"If the fire gets too hot, we'll put it in the indoor koi pond," I suggested. Jenny agreed that my idea made a lot of sense.

The fire, in fact, did get too hot when the toilet paper ignited like a Roman torch. We quickly doused it in the pond. About that time, one of the waitresses was heading down the stairs to grab a smoke. She got one all right, but it was the secondary smoke from our prank. And just like the fish, our goose was cooked.

As I recall, the koi turned a grayish color as they floated belly up in the indoor pond. That was the last family dinner we had and, if memory serves, it may have been the last time we ever saw our North Side relatives. I congratulated Jenny on her incredible "genius" once my phone privileges were restored, about six weeks later.

Jenny's brother Kenny also staged some memorable stunts. But the toilet paper caper reigned supreme and was the best-remembered event for years to come. It is noteworthy that our cousin from Highland Park did not participate in these questionable activities. While only eighteen months older than me, she had enough good sense to know that her younger South Side cousins were troublemakers. It took Jenny and me fifty years to establish a new relationship with her.

CHAPTER FIFTEEN

So, What's Doing at Pishler's Tonight?

A significant part of our lives in the Manor revolved around Jewish events, all of which led to the consumption of obscenely large amounts of food. Eating, cooking, feeding, or talking about food occupied virtually every moment of Manor life. Food seemed to be the central reason of our existence—in addition to playing Mahjong and listening to my Dad's disgusting jokes and racist diatribes.

The food obsession mysteriously correlated with becoming an adult, because as children we rarely ate more than peanut butter and jelly sandwiches, canned spaghetti, Kraft Mac and Cheese, Salerno Butter Cookies, vanilla wafers, and the occasional Fig Newton, but the Newtons only under duress.

"Eat," my mother daily begged me. "You look like a refugee."

But I refused to eat because food simply wasn't interesting, except for the Franco-American spaghetti and meatballs in a can with its runny orange sauce that seemed to be a staple in our home when my father was working. And Swanson's TV dinners, complete with fried chicken, mashed potatoes, peas, and some sort of hot, gooey dessert. But the spaghetti was my favorite. I painted pictures on my plate with that orange gelatinous goop. Mother's overcooked green vegetables were generally tucked in a neat circle under the edge of my dinner plate, or were handed to my dog, Tammy, who waited eagerly under the kitchen table.

I wasn't interested in eating beef tongue, kidneys, beet borscht, oxtails, sweetbreads, liver and onions, or questionable organ meats that were braised, broiled, boiled, or roasted.

My father, raised by his father as an Orthodox Jew, completely renounced his religious beliefs and occasionally glazed and baked a ham with cloves. He also asked my mom to fry pork chops for him. He picked apples from our tree in the backyard and made applesauce on occasion, graciously allowing my mother the opportunity to clean up the mess he made in the process. He even once attempted to tap our "maple tree" hoping to make homemade syrup, not realizing it was a Dutch elm.

I remained a scrawny little kid who ate very few things and yet somehow survived. Once a few years passed, however, the tonnage seemed to catch up with most of us. Marla said that when you turn 30, fat lumps somehow automatically grow on your hips, neck, stomach, and rear. She said she knew this to be true because her mother learned it in nursing school. And, of course, I believed everything Marla told me because she was my best friend and besides, she was almost a year older and therefore wiser.

Unfortunately, Marla was right. It truly seemed that fat molecules were electronically-charged little vectors somehow deployed to their anatomical targets by nuclear-powered missiles.

The almost inevitable gaining of weight was directly correlated with our Jewish lifecycle events. Not a week went by in which we weren't intimately relating to the rich, fatty foods of our ancestors. We Jews are always celebrating or mourning something. And what's a celebration or gathering without food? Our obsession with food is actually rooted in the Holy Covenant.

While cringing at our son David's bris (circumcision ceremony) and praying that the mohel wouldn't have a grand mal seizure while dicing David's foreskin on the eighth day of our son's life, I knew that very soon I would find solace, even as our beloved David howled. For just beyond the mohel's knife was the dining room where the real celebration would occur. And just as the sacred circumcision service celebrated our covenant with God, the heaping platters of chopped liver, noodle kugel, lox and bagels, and pickled herring symbolized our covenant with our caterers (and ultimately with our cardiologists and gastroenterologists). The South Side Jewish custom of eating, in fact, was a "womb to tomb" adventure.

My father died in Arizona in September 1991. He wished to be buried at the Jewish cemetery in Chicago where our other family members were interred, so we brought my father home on his final journey. Pishler's Chapel in Skokie seated over 300 of our family members and old family friends, all of whom paid their farewells to the man who told the filthiest jokes in Chicago. Pishler's was a happening place. It seemed like there wasn't a day that went by that we didn't have an intimate connection to one of Pishler's newly deceased.

Following the service and burial, seemingly everyone made their way to my cousin Jenny's house for a shiva, to pay their respects and, as Stu eloquently put it, "to follow their deviated septums to the feed lot."

As Sally Stackhouse, an old Manor friend, insightfully observed, "It was a Noodle Kugel Cook-off of such epic proportion that Betty Crocker (nee Crockerstein?) surely would have swooned had she still been alive." Noodle kugels with raisins, without raisins, with cinnamon and without, all things sweet and savory covered every flat surface in Jenny's kitchen. Had Dr. Seuss been present, a "Green Eggs and Kugel" book could have been written from the sheer magnitude of kugels that filled nearly every horizontal space in Jenny's home.

In the midst of our grief, a memorable gastronomic moment occurred when our son David, who was ten at the time, asked with real emotion: "Who had the nerve to bring chopped liver? Didn't Papa die from liver disease?"

"Oh my God," Jenny gasped. "Are you offended, Debbie? It didn't even occur to me."

Chopped liver, roast beef, corned beef, pastrami, egg salad, tuna salad, and sliced turkey are found on every deli platter at every Chicago-area shiva, along with kugels, an assortment of breads, lox and bagels, herring, salads, and condiments. Poor little David, an Arizona diaspora Jew, didn't know these traditions.

Stu and I laughed so hard we nearly had to spit out our food. This reaction both confused and angered David, who was very clearly insulted by the staggering mounds of olive-green chopped liver that he felt mocked his grandfather. From that moment on, my fondness for chopped liver was greatly diminished.

Stu insisted that new chins grew right before his eyes at the shiva meal for my father. Grief was well concealed behind overflowing plates of challah, cookies, halvah, and Entenmann's sweets, piled high on plates of the already-calorically-challenged.

David refused to eat.

While the after-Pishler food fests of the Manor no doubt added girth to many a waistline, nothing approached the wretched gastronomic excesses of bar mitzvah parties, those economic indicators of financial and social status. Stu calls the bar mitzvah party phenomenon the "true gastronomic Nasdaq indicator."

Planning bar mitzvah parties brought out the worst in everybody. Friends competed with friends to determine whose party would be the nicest, most unique, most elegant, and most sumptuously catered event. The problem on the South Side was that nobody had enough money to truly compete. The result was a stultifying sameness to the bar mitzvah parties of my youth. Nine parties out of ten were held in the ballroom of the Lake Shore Vistas Hotel, which forty years later is now the solarium of an assisted living center. I must have eaten 10 tons of rubbery, barely-roasted chicken during my thirteenth year.

In addition to chicken, you could count on there being overly baked potatoes, mushy peas and carrots, and still-frozen dinner rolls. The menu never varied from party to party. Adding to this monotony, the same musicians performed the same musical numbers without even varying their order. We knew precisely when "Hava Nagila" would be played in the lineup, along with "Cherish" and "Yesterday." Even our Serbian pal Dinky Kekich knew when we'd start dancing the hora.

If epidemiologists or coroners were to study Jewish Southsiders, they would likely find some remarkable similarities: diabetes was a way of life among M.O.T.s ("Members of the Tribe"), gallbladders blew like rockets on the Fourth of July, and chopped liver consumption was a leading indicator of the next arrivals to Pishler's.

Eating well beyond one's limits was just another "Manorism," as much a part as listening to the duplex neighbors argue through the common wall.

CHAPTER SIXTEEN

Through the Viaducts to James H. Bowen High School

There was one South Side structure that served as the central unifying place for Jews, Poles, Serbs, Croats, Mexicans, Greeks, Blacks, and Irish (and the byproducts of the few intermarriages thereof), and that was James H. Bowen High School. The formidable five-story fortress-like structure was built in 1911.

Who attended Bowen? High school students who did not attend Catholic high schools and who lived both north and south of the 95th Street viaducts, north to the Chicago Skyway at 83rd Street and south to 103rd Street, including those of us who resided in the Manor. Bowen's students were of all races, and many of us were Jewish, especially before 1972.

Railroad and roadway viaducts chopped our heterogeneous South Side into more homogeneous ethnic clusters. The Chicago Skyway, the universally-acknowledged "white elephant" toll road that linked Chicago to the eastern states, created an entire system of viaducts to the east of the Manor nearer the steel mills and Lake Michigan. The by-products of the Skyway were viaducts every few blocks, fragmenting the southeast portion of Chicago and effectively segregating ethnic groups. The Serbs, Croats, and Poles lived in a nearby little urban cluster, comprised largely of rickety three-flats and aging boxy bungalows close to the steel mills. These students also attended Bowen High School.

On the other side of one viaduct lived the Mexicans, Slavs and ethnic "others" of South Chicago. Shops in South Chicago were mainly geared to the ethnic tastes of those from south of the U.S. border. Interestingly, the largest shops in the neighborhood were owned by the Goldblatts, Lesters, and Gassmans, Jewish carpetbaggers who lived north of the Manor among the Jewish elite. The Jews from Pill Hill mostly shopped at Lesters and Gassmans, whereas the Mexicans, Poles, and Serbs usually frequented the much-lower-class Goldblatts and Three Sisters. My blue-collar family mostly shopped at the nearby Robert Hall.

Greeks were considered "almost Jews" and lived pretty much wherever they wanted. For some inexplicable reason, Greeks and Jews "clicked" on the South Side. In fact, many of our favorite restaurants were owned by guys named Spiro and Nick, where the busboys were often their sons and sons-in-law. Mr. Stavros Papagapoulos owned a great little ice cream parlor on Commercial Avenue. The Greeks could cook, and the Jews could eat, so it was a symbiosis made in heaven.

For the most part, the Irish lived in their own burgs to the west of us, closer to Ashland and Western. But the Manor also attracted a healthy population of lower middle-class Irish and Italian Catholics who lived side-by-side with Jews and the tiny minority of demographically indescribable "others."

Over time, Chicago's Blacks embarked on a southward progression, from the areas just south of the Chicago Loop into Kenwood, Hyde Park and, eventually, southward into South Shore, Chatham, Avalon Park, Marynook, Pill Hill, the Gardens, and, finally, south of the viaduct into the Manor.

The natural ethnic boundaries of the viaducts meant nothing to Chicago's Black citizens who understandably wanted to live in nicer, safer neighborhoods. One by one, as white neighbors fled from the integration, the signs of our venerated Manor restaurants, delis, clothing stores, and butchers came down and were replaced by new signs, smells, and purveyors of goods. Some of us were excited to live in an integrated neighborhood like Hyde Park and to learn about other races, cultures, and beliefs. But our collective willingness to coexist as neighbors didn't last long, fueled by innate fear and ignorance, intrinsic racism, and a simple lack of tolerance for traditions and attitudes too disparate from our own.

CHAPTER SEVENTEEN

A Bad Case of Writer's Ego at Bowen High School

My first attempt at a novel began when I was a creative writing student at Bowen High. It opened with these words:

> "She was certain for most of her life of her higher gifts of insight and inspired thinking. It is my story, 'Mysterium Delirium' deliciously, delectably enshrouded in fantasies of the magnitude that truly amaze even myself."

My high school creative writing teacher walked out of the room after I read that passage aloud. She did not return to class that day, as I recall.

Nonplussed but idealistic, I dreamed my book jacket would include this rave review:

> "A wonderful read—a sinewy tale of soul-searching, meaning-seeking, teeth-gritting, spiritual desert walks through the shadows of the valley of enlightenment in the Higher Power."
>
> *Literary Monthly*

And this:

> "Pithy. An enlightened inspiration for each of us caught up in the spiral of self-doubt." *The New Yorker*

But the jacket really should have read:

"Self-indulgent, metaphorical poop of the highest vintage with a rotting bouquet intolerable to most nostrils."
Mike Royko, *The Chicago Sun-Times*

An aspiring journalist, I became a writer on our high school newspaper, the *Bowen Arrow*, the publication that propelled me into journalism school at the University of Illinois. Fortunately, my high school journalism teacher, Ms. Schwarzkopf, detected a tiny glimmer of raw potential. Dedicated soul that she was, she taught me how to write a simple sentence.

Bowen High School produced some of the most talented and driven kids of our generation. Bowen's Jews were virtually all college bound. The more affluent and successful graduates ended up at schools such as Yale, Cornell, Colgate, Carlton, Oberlin, Case Western Reserve, and Brandeis. Few of the Manor's Jews, however, made it much farther than the state universities located in Chicago, Urbana-Champaign, DeKalb, and Carbondale, not for a lack of ability but rather for a lack of funds to underwrite private colleges and out-of-state tuition. Nonetheless, we were pleased with our accomplishments and we were aware that our parents were prouder still.

Bowen High School was a model for the United Nations, a colorful crazy quilt of virtually every racial and ethnic group that made its way through Ellis Island and other ports of entry in the last century. For the most part, we hung with our own cohorts. The Jewish kids and a few of our non-Jewish friends generally were placed in honors classes, while most of the "assorted other students" rarely made it out of remedial or basic classes. Several Greeks took honors classes with the Jews.

Many of Bowen's Jewish students were members of clubs sponsored by B'nai B'rith, an international Jewish organization. Girls were in B'nai B'rith Girls or "BBG" chapters and boys were in Aleph Zadik Aleph or "AZA" chapters. Each chapter consisted of about 30 members and was characterized by its respective level of "coolness" as well as its originating neighborhood. For example, I was a member of Tovah BBG, with membership mostly composed of Bowenites from the

Manor. Many of the guys I knew were members of Manor AZA, the self-proclaimed "Mighty Manor Men." The coolest girls were in Negev BBG. The coolest guys were in Fort Dearborn AZA.

Each year, BBGs from all over Chicagoland (District 6) competed in various activities in juried competitions called "Invite." We competed in such activities as song, dance, oratory, storytelling, volleyball, table tennis, and others. The culmination of the annual Invite competitions—akin to the Olympics—was a formal dance at a large downtown hotel. We began the evenings with pre-dinner gatherings. Then we'd drive to the hotel ballrooms for the dance and attend late-night fancy dinners at restaurants and after-dance parties at one of our homes. Those too young to drive often double dated with slightly older couples. Most of us were breaking curfew, with the permission of our parents. One year, my date was picked up for a curfew violation after he dropped me off at my home. Around 3 a.m. we heard from Paul's parents that he had been taken to the South Chicago Police Station.

The AZA chapters also had annual Invite competitions, with competing categories and formal dances. These were big deals, and we would spend the day getting our hair done and getting dolled up in our fancy new dresses for these annual galas.

The identities of BBG and AZA chapters were often denoted by our outfits of choice. For example, the girls of Tovah BBG selected a preppy look with plum-colored crewneck sweaters worn over light-blue blouses, navy-blue skirts and navy-blue knee socks, and penny loafers. We wore navy blue and white baseball-style jackets that clearly read "Tovah BBG" on the back. These clothes signaled our group identities and gave us a sense of tribal belongingness.

We proudly wore our Tovah jackets in the warmer weather, but we were a small part of the overall potpourri of multi-ethnic and multi-racial students, many of whom sported their own identifying symbolic clothing.

The great levelers of all ethnic and racial groups at Bowen High School in the 1960s were the P.E. classes, homeroom, and lunch periods in the cavernous cafeteria. In these places, privileged white honors students coexisted but rarely mingled with students from neighborhoods cut off from theirs by the viaducts. We knew the Serbs, Poles, and Croats, but we usually sat in our own corners of the rooms, rarely made eye contact, and didn't socialize or try to piss them off.

West Side Story had its Jets and Sharks and their often-lethal rumbles. Similarly, when attendance was taken in homeroom at Bowen High School on Monday mornings, we would learn which ethnic or racial gangs reigned supreme in weekend wars along with the names of their latest victims. It was daunting to hear the name of a classmate who had been a weekend warrior in a gang war, now dead. Most rumbles seemed to occur between Mexican and warring Black gangs, although we heard unsubstantiated rumors about feuds among Serbs, Croatians and Mexicans.

One common lunchroom activity that transcended ethnic and racial lines though was the sport of throwing forks into the acoustic tiles in the cafeteria's ceiling. Those seated at the Serbian tables were most successful, with the greatest number of forks dangling menacingly over plates of greasy cheeseburgers and bowls of chili. These were Bowen's star "athletes."

Life changed at Bowen the moment Martin Luther King, Jr., was assassinated. On that day, the Negro students at Bowen became "Afros" and with their new identity and growing numbers, they also became increasingly militant and noticeably less tolerant of white students. A Black-sponsored sit-in in the high school cafeteria the day after King's assassination resulted in our sophomore class becoming hostages, as the cafeteria was where we had homeroom.

It was several hours before Chicago policemen arrived to liberate the white students. On that day, timid white Jewish kids walked home together in large numbers. This was a precipitous event on Chicago's South Side, a scary and surreal experience for previously-sheltered white fifteen-year-olds. It also sparked the beginning of the white exodus from Bowen High School. It was a defining moment.

"For Sale" signs quickly began appearing in Jewish-centric neighborhoods on both sides of the viaduct, although the neighborhoods north of the viaduct transitioned at an even faster pace. Bowen's

Jews mainly fled to Skokie and other suburbs north of downtown Chicago, or south to Homewood, Flossmoor, and Glenwood. As another measure of this exodus, Bowen's Class of 1970 dwindled from 1,200 students in 1966 to about 800 by 1970. A much smaller group of stalwart Jews remained on the South Side for our graduation at Medinah Temple.

The Jewish girls of Tovah BBG, my close high school friends, parted ways by 1971, as the vast majority were no longer living in the area. By 1969–70, during my high school years, the once-thriving cultural magnet for South Side Jewish families—the Jewish Community Center (JCC) north of the viaduct—morphed into the site of a depressing weekly wake to count the ghosts of our friends who'd fled during the prior weeks to new homes in the suburbs.

Bowen High School produced many memories: a swimming pool with water the consistency of extra-firm-hold Dippity-Doo, greasy olive-green lockers, steamy hot hallways even in mid-January, anti-Semitic spitballs directed at us from our not-so-admiring Polish and Mexican classmates, and weekend knife fights between Mexicans and Blacks that routinely whittled away their numbers.

Bowen High School was also the focal point of Jews from both sides of the viaduct. Most of the Manor kids couldn't afford to keep up with the fashions worn by our friends north of the viaduct. We shopped at Lerner's and Stuart's at Evergreen Park Plaza, while our friends to the north shopped at Marshall Field's, Steven's, and Carson's. The cool and mostly wealthy Jewish kids pledged high school fraternities and sororities. The "less cool" Jewish teens joined the AZA and BBG chapters at Bowen. The really talented teens (like my cousin Jenny, our "honorary Jewish" Manor friend Fred, and others) starred in teen theater musicals at the JCC and derived their primary identities through Teen Theater.

There were so many Jews at Bowen that social stratification was very much a part of our high school experience. A pecking order was somehow imposed on every Jewish kid at Bowen. Our parents' money and professional accomplishments probably influenced where we landed on this "hierarchy of social acceptability," along with a few other variables. My cousin Jenny, Marla, and her older sister Jackie reached the nirvana of acceptance by the popular Jews from north of the viaduct. Marla was beautiful, smart, kind, and personable. Her rise was no small feat and clearly an accomplishment with zero correlation to the funds in her family's checkbook. Jenny was popular, attractive, and extremely talented. She became close friends with members of the JCC teen theater and dated two wealthy "north of the viaduct" guys in high school.

What for me is most memorable about Bowen High School? Mr. Angelo Magnavite, for one. He was our sleek and stylish Spanish teacher who stimulated our competitive juices with our mad blackboard dashes to conjugate Spanish verbs in exchange for credits. Angelo Magnavite: the words rolled deliciously in the mouth and tickled our budding little libidos. What a man!

The Class of 1970 was fortunate to enjoy Bowen's beautiful new addition that mysteriously appeared at precisely the time the white population was taking flight. I remember gym classes in Bessemer Park, an urban patch of weeds shared with the park's resident winos, drug addicts, and homeless sailors from the nearby docks. I recall Stu's numerous muggings by Bowen's Blacks, Poles, Mexicans, and Serbs. I fondly remember our sophomore music class taught by a mincing gay Black teacher ("Aida, Aida, glory, glory, Aida," he sang out to the wrong crowd) who received absolutely no mercy from any of us. It was in this very classroom where I frequently plucked spitballs (one-part saliva, one-part Kleenex, and two-parts vapid spite) from my thick hair thanks to the marksman-like accuracy of Valerie Hidalgo, one of our school's perpetual sophomores. Valerie was one of South Chicago's finest, a giant with a pea-sized brain, whose other significant sophomore achievements included pushing me down a flight of stairs for being a "fucking, rich Jew girl." My conclusion, almost fifty years later, is that Valerie must have perceived me to be a privileged Jewish *white* girl.

Jewish students were easy targets at Bowen. Stu, a student of relatively short stature, started carrying his lunch and bus money in his shoe after being frequently rolled by taller students from various ethnic and racial groups. My locker in my junior P.E. class was broken into and my purse was stolen. I later found my purse in a trashcan outside of Bowen—without my wallet but with most of my other possessions intact.

Most of all, I will never forget the great days and wonderful friendships made at Bowen High School. Or the heartbreak of watching our friends move away, seemingly overnight, to enroll in suburban high schools that were then immune to the societal ripple effects from the death of Martin Luther King, Jr.

CHAPTER EIGHTEEN

God's Little Miracle: Mormons in Yarmulkes

I took the Miller Analogies Test many years ago as a prerequisite for admission into a master's degree program in communications. I think the test is supposed to test one's ability to make word associations, comparisons, and contrasts. Since I guessed on virtually every analogy when taking that test many years ago, I guess I'll never really know the point.

Now for an analogy: Debbie is to the Manor as:

A) Mormons in yarmulkes are to the Low's annual Passover seder in Arizona.

B) Mormons in yarmulkes are at Sally Sackhouse's seder in Glenview.

C) Mormons who sing songs about pioneers but who don't wear yarmulkes.

D) Mormons who neither drink Mogen David Concord Wine nor wear yarmulkes.

Let's guess and go with "A" for this one.

Sandy Sackhouse, the slightly younger twin sister of Sally Sackhouse, now of Glenview, Illinois, briefly flew back into my life after a twenty-five-year hiatus to share the magic of our Passover seder. Why was this night different from all other nights? Let us now recall answer A: *Mormons in Yarmulkes.*

Our son David, then a lifelong resident of Arizona, lived a far different teenaged experience than Sandy, Sally, Stu, and I did at Bowen. David knew nothing of Jewish pecking orders nor of kids named Howard, Benjamin, Bruce, Mark, Michael, Stevie, Sam, or Moshe. But oh, that Brigham Young!

David's world was filled with Nordic-looking, young men with first names like Cameron, Travis, Taylor, Branden, and Preston—great looking, sweet-acting guys en route to two years of Mormon missionary work, to be followed by predictable marriages to obedient Mormon wives who would beget enough young Mormons to fill a Chevy Suburban. It was these great young men who collectively made our seder the most wonderful ever. David's true buddies cherished him with every ounce of genuine male affection.

In the spirit of pure friendship, five strapping young Mormon high school boys wearing yarmulkes joined our family and friends in a real celebration of freedom and liberty from the shackles of slavery. And Sandy Sackhouse joined us to witness a seder meal delightfully different from most.

David and his buddies laughed hysterically as Travis chewed off a large chunk of raw horseradish on a dare and proclaimed it "The best bitter herb I ever ate." Trav's face turned a brilliant shade of crimson from the heat of the root. Imagine five tall boys—and one short, dark-haired Jewish kid named David among them—searching for the afikoman while wearing yarmulkes of turquoise, magenta, green and pink. And then to have the discoverer of the afikomen be the next boy to leave on his Mormon mission to Chile. The spirit of the seder was joyful like no other, partly inspired by this band of beanied boys, and by the presence of a former Manorite, Sandy. Together we returned to our high school state of mind, from a time long before the endless challenges of becoming achingly adult.

CHAPTER NINETEEN

No Money, but Who Cares?

When you grow up south of the viaduct, there are a few things you don't have from the very beginning, starting with money. Your friends from the other side of the viaduct do not come to your house. Why? Because they're truly afraid about what happens south of the viaduct, especially after Richard Speck's night of infamy.

But there were many other things that we had in great abundance. We had, for example, access to swamps (toxic landfill with contaminated wastewater) that would overgrow in the summer months with cattails (called "punks") that we smoked. You could ride your bike to the swamp and look for rodents, lizards, tadpoles, snakes, rabbits, squirrels, and frogs. Some of my friends ice skated on the frozen swampland. Occasional tramps who rode the rails above the viaduct could also be found in the swamp, generally regarded by neighborhood hobos to be a choice hangout. If the wind blew just right, you could climb atop a landfill hill and catch the deep-fried air currents drifting from the nearby Jay's Potato Chip factory. Some of my friends smoked pot for the first time in the swamp with our high school biology teacher on a "field trip."

We also had Kiddy Land, west of the Manor, bordering the swamp. It had some great rides like the Santa Fe miniature train, Mad Mouse roller coaster, a merry-go-round, a small Ferris wheel, the Rock-O-Planes, the Paratrooper, the Round-Up, the Octopus, Swinging Gym, and hand-cranked rail cars. Our parents took us there when we were little. I remember the time my dog Lady jumped into one of the little floating boats when it started thundering and lightning. As we got older, we played on their miniature golf course and drove their go-karts. In the seventh and eighth grades, we hung out at Kiddy Land where we made out with our boyfriends.

In the Manor, we could ride our bikes in places we were allowed to go and some places we weren't supposed to go, like south along Doty past the incinerator and near the sanitation canal. We could watch old men bait their hooks to fish for chemically mutated catfish and hunt for skunk, and we could pretend that we were on an adventure. After a long bike ride, we could stop at Groceryland to see if the shipment of Yoo-hoo (the chocolate drink in a bottle) had arrived.

We were allowed to ride our bikes to Merrill Park and to Yates Park (aka Bensley Park), where in the winter we'd skate on a well-maintained ice-skating rink. When the ice conditions were perfect, we'd even ice skate in the street in front of my house.

Near my house, we could hang out at Pinzur's Pharmacy where we could get the latest installments of Archie and Veronica, Superman, and Batman comic books. They'd even ignore us and let us read the comics for free if we'd buy a handful of Bazooka Joe bubblegum or a Drumstick.

Slagle's was the place to find a little of this and a little of that, from 12-cent "real" birthstone rings with adjustable bands to new school supplies each September. In that same strip mall, you could buy delicious cookies and cakes at the Swedish bakery, have your heels fixed and your shoes polished, buy a new pair of PF Flyers, pick up a new garden hose at the Manor Ace Hardware Store, bowl at DeVito's Lanes next to the Chinese restaurant, and buy your groceries at the National. Or you could walk a little farther west on 95th Street to the A&P, W.T. Grant (the place to buy live baby turtles and ugly blue gym suits for high school), Baskin-Robbins (by the way, when they opened, a single scoop was little more than a dime), Key Club Cleaners, and Hillman's grocery store.

Topps Restaurant on 95th Street was owned by a Jewish family from the Manor. We often went there for French fries with rich brown gravy, vanilla Cokes, "Mile High Sundaes," and a free sucker from the lollipop tree. It was at Topp's that I first discovered how much I liked onion rings.

Walgreen's was on the southeast corner of 95th and Jeffery, home to pints of affordable ice cream, medicine, and seemingly every item under the sun. For a long time, I didn't realize there was more than one Walgreen's. I was shocked when I discovered others in our travels!

Around the corner on Jeffery was Bergman's, a kosher-style deli just south of 95th Street, along with a few other stores including Bell's for relatively expensive girls' clothes, Charold's shoe store, and a nursery school. Later, Pic 'N' Save moved in with all kinds of cheap junk (referred to by my father as *chazeri*—Yiddish for cheap junk).

Mostly, we could do lots of really great things south of the viaduct and, fortunately, very few of them required more than a couple of dimes and a bike.

Those of us from the viaduct's southern side were privy to neither the affluence nor the affectations associated with wealth. We were the children of mothers whose "good tablecloths" were made of vinyl with an inset of vinyl lace trim. We knew of Naugahyde; we knew nothing of leather. But over time, we learned.

CHAPTER TWENTY

Phoenix: A Suburb of Western Chicago

When Stu and I moved to Arizona in 1979, we were astounded by the large number of Chicagoans we met virtually everywhere we went. Old Chicagoans, young Chicagoans. Middle-aged Chicagoans. You can easily tell, as we all sound very much the same.

What is it about Arizona that draws Chicagoans of all ages and backgrounds? In part, it is Arizona State University in Tempe and the University of Arizona in Tucson, popular state universities for Chicago-area students. Clearly, in the wintertime, it is our lovely weather. But in the summer, it's horrifyingly hot here, at least until our annual monsoon season brings an ever-so-slight cooldown along with massive dust storms, thunderstorms, and flash floods.

It certainly isn't the food that attracts Chicagoans to Arizona. Until recently, with the arrival of Lou Malnati's and Giordano's, you couldn't find a really good Chicago pan pizza in Arizona to save your soul, although Oregano's came the closest. A Chicago hot dog with snap in a poppy seed bun with mustard, bright green relish, raw onions, and celery salt is a pleasant encounter. (We now have Portillo's Hot Dogs, a Chicago transplant, and their dogs do have snap!) We had Uno's branches, but they were awful and ultimately fizzled. A Gino's East satellite in Tempe and later in Phoenix were equally bad and both closed after a couple of years. I mean, if you can't do it right, why bother?

The only real "Arizona" cuisine comes from south of the border. One can find hundreds of Mexican, Tex-Mex, and New Mexican-inspired restaurants throughout the state, most with gloppy cheese and beans, requiring a chaser of Tums.

A phenomenon that Stu and I experienced is the growing of kidney stones in the desert Southwest. Apparently, we Chicago ex-pats become dehydrated, which contributes to kidney issues. In looking for a nearby urologist, I stumbled on the name of Dr. Samuel Greenberg in nearby Tempe. "Is he a M.O.T.? Probably. Let's give him a try."

As it happened, Dr. Greenberg displayed a University of Illinois diploma on his wall. "Where are you from?" I inquired. "Chicago," replied Dr. Greenberg. "What part of Chicago?" "South Side." "What high school?" "Bowen," he answered.

Upon further questioning, he revealed that he grew up two blocks away from where my husband did, and that they attended the same elementary school. We all attended Bowen High School and the University of Illinois. Dr. Greenberg was 13 years older than we were, and he looked like he could be Stu's older brother. His bar mitzvah was held at the South Shore temple that employed the rabbi who married my parents. We also learned that Dr. Greenberg worked during medical school at the same millinery company as my mother.

We later met the Greenbergs at a social gathering of another Jewish urologist friend of ours. After some pleasantries, we found out that Dr. Greenberg's wife Chrissy grew up on Chicago's North Side, and also had a mother who moved to Arizona to be near them. We vowed to introduce our mothers, but it never happened.

One day, my mother called and said she'd met a woman named Lolly at her weekly Mahjong game at the Tempe senior center, a lady from the North Side who wanted to learn how to play. "She doesn't look Jewish," my mother said. Nonetheless, my mother welcomed her to the group and, over time, a friendship developed. One day, my phone rang and my mother sang out, "You'll never believe it! My new Mahjong friend from Chicago is your friend Chrissy Greenberg's mother!" Chrissy received a similar call from her mom, Lolly. From that time until the deaths of my mom, Lolly and Chrissy, our Chicago diaspora flourished and the Greenbergs became an integral and much-loved part of our Arizona family.

A few years ago, the Chicago Cubs built an amazing new spring training facility just east of Arizona State University, "south of the river." And Stu, stalwart South Sider that he is, still hates the Chicago Cubs (who hail from the North Side) as much as he did in high school. He is, forever and truly, a fan of the Chicago White Sox, the only professional ball team on the city's South Side. In fact, Stu's lifelong dislike for the Cubs is so intense that he refuses to set foot in this magnificent spring training stadium. Ironically, the Chicago White Sox hold their spring training north of the river in Scottsdale.

Chicagoans seem to be *everywhere* in Arizona. Our Arizona next-door neighbors still own a home on the farthest reaches of the South Side near 130th and Torrence. Another grew up on the southwest side of Chicago and remembers shopping at my father's little store at 111th and Kedzie. Two years older than we are, she also was a graduate of the University of Illinois. Others we have met here grew up on the North Side and continue to retain their strong sense of being Chicagoans.

Robin, a former Manor friend, moved to Tempe with her family in 1969, a year before we were to graduate from Bowen. At that time, none of us had ever heard of Tempe. Robin was genuinely sad about leaving the Manor and her Bowen boyfriend behind. Many years later, we discovered in the local newspaper that Robin was a physics professor at a community college in nearby Chandler. We invited Robin and her family for brunch. Not long after that brunch, we learned that Robin died from pancreatic cancer at a very young age. Her sisters, whom I didn't know, reportedly still reside in the area.

One of the strangest Manor coincidences occurred a year after I retired from my psychotherapy practice in Chandler. I was invited to a holiday party hosted by a fellow therapist who owned the building where I had leased my former office. I knew most of the people at the party, but a few new tenants appeared. I sat with Helene, a woman approximately my age whom I didn't know. She told me that she, too, was a therapist in the building and that she was originally from Chicago.

Like any true Chicagoan, the first question I asked was, "From what part of the city?" The typical answer would be "South Side," "North Side," "West Side," "East Side," or "the suburbs." Helene responded, "South Side."

The next inevitable question: "What high school did you attend?" Helene responded, "Bowen, not far from Lake Michigan." I told her that I, too, attended Bowen. She said she graduated in 1969 and I told her I graduated in 1970. I asked her what neighborhood she grew up in and she said, "The Manor." My response: "So did I!"

As it turned out, Helene grew up across the street from my old school chum, Felice, with whom she'd remained close friends. To make an already small world even smaller, Helene's mother played Mahjong with my mother, and Helene's father was our TV repairman. In fact, he was virtually every Manorite's TV repairman. It also turned out that Helene and I attended the same ultra-Reform temple in Hyde Park.

But wait! The story gets stranger still. It turns out that Helene's Manor neighbor, Felice, knew my husband Stu practically from the day he was born. Both hailed from German-Jewish families and both families landed in the same apartment building in Hyde Park. Felice is two months older than Stu. Both families attended the same German-Jewish synagogue in South Shore. And Helene, Stu, and I attended Felice's bat mitzvah party at the South Chicago YMCA, although we didn't know each other at the time.

And there's more. Felice and I went on to the University of Illinois at Urbana-Champaign and lived in the same dorm our freshman year. Felice roomed with Helen, another Manor friend, and I roomed with Joan, my best friend from Bowen. We all knew each other. The twin dorms of the Florida Avenue Residence Halls (one for men and the other for women) housed many Manorites over the years and became a comfortable respite from our little Chicago enclave that, by then, was becoming a predominantly Black neighborhood. Stu transferred his sophomore year from Oberlin to the University of

Illinois, against his parents' wishes to keep us apart. Stu also ended up in the Florida Avenue Residence Hall, another South Sider in exile. You couldn't go anywhere on the campus of the University of Illinois at Urbana- Champaign without running into a Manorite or Bowen alumnus. We were everywhere! While the proximity of people like us was comforting during our freshman year, by the time we were better adjusted to life away from our roots, we were ready to leave many of our old acquaintances behind.

CHAPTER TWENTY-ONE

Planning Our 50th High School Reunion

"Ahhhhh," moaned Stu, sounding convincingly ill. "Please don't make me go to our fiftieth high school reunion. There is absolutely nobody I want to see."

"Nobody?" I inquired. "Not a single human being—other than those I already keep in touch with," he answered.

He was referring to a group which was comprised only of my best friend, Joan; my rediscovered friend, Barbara; and her husband, David (with whom we double-dated to our senior prom). Stu and Barbara attended elementary school, high school, and college together, but had lost touch.

"Nobody?" I queried again.

"Nobody," said Stu, this time with emphasis.

"Well," I said, "I want to go. So, we'll go."

I should explain that Stu is not antisocial. He's not a hermit. In fact, he is a very funny, very witty guy. Almost everyone loves Stu. He's intelligent, caring, kind, and extremely good-natured. He has many wonderful traits, and is the most moral and ethical person I have ever known. Bar none.

Stu is, very simply, not nostalgic. It's not a fault. It's just that the past holds absolutely no significance in his schema of life's meaning. Most of his memories of growing up include bad religious school experiences with ethically challenged rabbis, various forms of torture by malicious neighborhood bullies, mediocre teachers, and mean-spirited adults, many of whom were his relatives or mine.

His memories of "the good old days" include being hazed by a few gigantic oafs in his elementary school, primarily due to his short, once-pudgy stature, his nerdiness, and his two formerly silver-capped front teeth (gained after some kid tripped him knocking out his two front permanent teeth, which were thankfully replaced by natural-looking crowns by the time I met him).

I first became aware of Stu in our sophomore high school honors physics class that included an assortment of geeks, math whizzes, bright kids and me—smart enough but lacking any advanced math skills. My earliest positive memory of Stu was his graciousness in passing his physics exam paper around the class for the benefit of a few of us who had no business being placed in an honors physics class since we lacked the necessary math background. Fortunately, our physics teacher (an elderly Charlie Weaver lookalike with a clear case of post-stroke dementia) was clueless about what was happening right under his nose.

Despite Stu's geekiness, he appeared to have compassion for those of us who flew into genuine panic attacks when attempting to determine voltages in circuits.

Unfortunately, fifteen-year-old Stu was still physically immature and a fawning teacher's-pet-sort-of-guy who was of little interest to most teenage girls.

Stu had friends—good friends—a couple of whom later served as best man and groomsman at our wedding. One went on to become a cardiologist, the other an endodontist. (These guys and a few of their other pals could have easily inspired the creation of the characters Sheldon, Leonard, Howard, and Raj on the popular TV show *The Big Bang Theory*.)

While I benefited from Stu's kindness, I was turned off by his geekiness. I really didn't think of him at all until our senior year when we were classmates in an honors English class. What I noticed about Stu at that time was that he had changed a lot from the fifteen-year-old version I once knew. He looked more mature. He had grown up and was nice looking.

As fate would have it, his closest friend—the one who became the endodontist—wanted his girlfriend (my friend) to sleep over at his mother's new suburban home on New Year's Eve of our senior year. But my friend couldn't go unless I went, too. The proviso was that I would go along as Stu's "date." We would all spend the night at his friend's suburban house, playing games, hanging out, and celebrating the coming New Year.

Since I wasn't in a relationship at that point and had no plans for New Year's Eve, I finally agreed to go after much pleading from my friend. What I hadn't anticipated was the sudden departure of our friends to his bedroom, and the subsequent hours of time spent sitting on the floor with Stu as we got to know each other.

Another thing I hadn't anticipated was that I'd discover I genuinely liked Stu. A lot. He was a kind and funny guy. He was easy to talk to. We shared some interests. And it was clear that he liked me, too.

The New Year's Eve experiment was a success, presumably for all four of us. Stu and I had a great time, even though we spent very little of it with our friends (or maybe *because* they weren't around). Either way, Stu and I started seeing a lot of each other in 1970, and it wasn't long before he asked me on a date. It was billed as a "study date" to the downtown Chicago library and later to see a matinee showing of "Cactus Rose." We had a fun day together.

And then, he blew it.

In mid-January 1970, probably due to his inexperience and cluelessness, he asked me to go with him to our senior prom. While I was flattered by his early invitation, I wasn't ready to commit to going to prom with Stu if a "relationship" with him might not last to May. So, I broke his heart.

I met him at my locker to break the news to him that I didn't see a future for us as a couple. I gave him the classic "Let's be friends" line. Stu's reaction was genuinely understanding. Later that evening, he called and thanked me for my honesty. We talked. And we talked. And talked some more. For almost three hours. After that, we continued to spend time together with the agreement that we'd put the prom discussion on hold.

Come May of 1970, Stu and I attended our senior prom as a couple.

As I've written earlier, Bowen High School had a very strong caste system. Overall, the smart kids were all in the same honors classes. At Bowen, most of these students were Jewish, Greek, or a few assorted demographic "others." Within this system, the honors student contingent also had its spectrum of losers, geeks/nerds, middle-of-the-packers, moderately cool, and very cool kids.

Where did I fall on that spectrum? I was clearly a middle-of-the-packer in terms of coolness, and I knew it. We middle-of-the-packers had our own cliques, our own friends, our own clubs, our own way of being. We generally were bright, college-bound, moderately well-adjusted teens with a sense of belonging in a comfortable niche. We were "good kids" in that we avoided alcohol and drugs, sex, and doing bad stuff like stealing ("hocking") makeup from W. T. Grant and Walgreen's.

What made the cool kids cool? I honestly don't know. Most weren't student athletes. (Those were most often Serbians, Croatians, Poles, Mexicans, and Black students.) White honors students didn't even go to Bowen sports activities for fear of getting beaten up.

Starting in seventh grade and continuing through high school years, the cool kids ruled, dazzled, and intimidated the rest of us. The way the Manor schools were situated, three "feeder" schools provided education from kindergarten through sixth grade to children in the outer reaches of the neighborhood. The feeder schools sent their students in seventh and eighth grades to our larger elementary school. We often didn't know many of these other Manor kids until they invaded our hallways, although we had met some of them at the local synagogue and in scout troops.

They were often the first ones on the dance floor at our weekly socials. The rest of us held our collective breaths with the hope we might be asked to dance by a boy from our place on the social spectrum. The cool girls were self-confident, secure in their status. Some of them were stuck up, believing they were too cool to be seen with the rest of us. They danced with cool boys, many of whom were, quite honestly, dimwits. They wore makeup, made out with the cool boys, and some (reportedly) went all the way.

Stu's elementary school had a similar social hierarchy. Many of his classmates matriculated to Bowen High School just before they moved to the suburbs. Stu, being firmly entrenched with the braniac nerds at his elementary school, and later at Bowen, had zero interest in or chance of seeking validation from the cool kids at school. He never gave it two thoughts. Quite simply, and to his credit, he didn't care.

After we graduated from eighth grade, Manorites from the Bowen classes of 1969 through 1971 began high school at a "branch campus" on the first floor of our elementary school. We didn't have an authentic high school experience until our sophomore year when we moved to Bowen's main campus. By then, some of our friends were already moving out of the neighborhood as a result of the early wave of white flight.

The cool kids from the Manor generally couldn't keep up financially with the cool kids from the other side of the viaduct. The great reckoning came when the cool Manorites met the cool kids from north of the viaduct during our sophomore year in high school. It became less clear who was "in" and who was "out," although the boundaries of coolness still were not breached by anyone outside the elite. And with the exodus of whites fully in progress, fewer cliques remained intact.

Joan and I mostly hung out with a small group of smart, Jewish, middle-of-the-packers in local BBG chapters. It became quite clear that one of our closest friends desperately sought to be accepted by the cool group residing north of the viaduct where she and my other close friends in high school lived. She lived in one of the smaller houses on Pill Hill. Relatively speaking, her family had some measure of affluence. She desperately sought validation, acceptance, and admission into the league of coolness, only to be forced to hang out with us. After a typical teenage falling out, Joan and I lost touch with her, although we had occasional glimpses of her at the University of Illinois.

And this is part of the conundrum of the Bowen Class of '70

reunion. Who are the main organizers? The cool white kids from the feeder schools or the kids we didn't really associate with from north of the viaduct? Did they even know who we were? Will there be enough of us former "middle of the packers" and nerds to actually enjoy the evening or will we feel marginalized once more? Is it worth the effort to fly to Chicago, to bear the financial and emotional costs of seeing people we didn't even know all that well fifty years ago?

People move on. We certainly did, and we brought very few of our former classmates along for the ride.

In the past twenty-five years, Manor reunions started happening at the funerals of our parents, relatives, former neighbors, and their kids. We've gathered to grieve, to remember, to eat, to laugh, to cry, and to tell stories. We've celebrated the lives of those who passed and then, after saying our goodbyes, continued to live our lives in the present tense, rarely in the company of those we once lived near.

(Full disclosure: I still rely on Marla to bring me up to date on Manor gossip. The Manor women—formerly our mothers and now our own generation of aging "kids"—regularly get together to catch up and keep each other informed about new developments.)

Our parents are long departed and now more of our contemporaries and their children are dying. Not from the Vietnam War and drug overdoses that took some lives in the 1970s, but from later-acquired cancers, heart attacks, suicides, and other causes. Death is now hitting our generation: our former neighbors, our classmates, our friends, and our families. Add to this the horrendous toll inflicted by the raging Coronavirus pandemic.

One former Bowen classmate, an emeritus finance professor at Penn State, expressed his excitement about our upcoming 50th reunion. "Count me in," he texted. A month later, however, another classmate informed us on Facebook of his sudden, unexpected death.

Another childhood friend from the Manor was diagnosed with inoperable lung cancer. As her disease rapidly progressed, she became a hospice patient, dependent on oxygen twenty-four seven. As her pain and discomfort intensified, she fully accepted her fate. She died six months after receiving her diagnosis. When learning the news about our friend's terminal illness, an online support group of former classmates coalesced to support her as she fought the disease. Some of us are now back in touch after many years apart. Most of us know very little about the lives, livelihoods, lifestyles, and specifics of our former friends since we last met. But we shared powerful memories with our struggling friend, and shared an expressed hope for a peaceful outcome for her.

Several persons I know from the Manor, including some of my classmates, have been treated for cancers. My old pal Marky fought prostate cancer and lymphoma and seems to be doing quite well. Sadly, he lost his wife, an alumna from the Bowen Class of '71, a couple of years ago to a particularly virulent form of metastatic cancer.

Other Bowen buddies are struggling with other cancers, COPD, early onset dementia, and other assorted diseases. Some have expressed their current fear of traveling in "petri dishes" to attend the reunion while COVID-19 continues unabated. Stu and I are in that group.

Still others are enjoying life to the fullest and are eager to share their memories, stories, and successes with the group.

Bowen Class of '70—Reunion or Bust? As I finish writing this chapter, I can only say swallow a few Xanax and tune in.

Epilogue

hiraeth

(n.) a homesickness for a home to which you cannot return, a home which maybe never was; the nostalgia, the yearning, the grief for the lost place of your past

pronunciation | ʻhEr-rIth (HEER-eyeth)

WELSH

As it turned out, *none* of us made it to our 50th High School Reunion in 2020. Life always has a way of happening, even when we have other plans. COVID-19 illnesses and deaths derailed our 50th celebration, but we are hopeful for another opportunity to get together in the future.

But even before that we knew we wouldn't be there. In our case, our much beloved English cocker spaniel, Wimsey Joy, was stricken with acute renal failure in December 2019. After two weeks of herculean attempts to bring her back to her sweet, nearly twelve-year-old doggy self, we knew her days were numbered. We opted for a peaceful and respectful ending before she experienced pain or discomfort. On December 23rd, we bade a tearful farewell to our very favorite dog of all time. Oh, how we loved her!

It has been a gut-wrenching grief. Wimsey was my constant

companion at home in Arizona (when Stu and I were not visiting Ellie, our beautiful granddaughter in Fresno, or traveling elsewhere). Ellie often greeted Wimsey on Facetime chats when we checked in with her. Ellie's almost four now and asks if Wimsey is in heaven ("Yes!") followed by "Is Wimsey feeling better?" (Also, "Yes!").

Wimsey was an equal opportunity lover. She adored us, happy to cuddle, lie on us, and shadow us from room to room. She frequently followed me into the walk-in shower in our master bathroom to drink water and be a part of the experience. Wimsey enjoyed being my bathroom companion and accompanied me to our large master closet to help me select my clothing.

We discussed the freedom of not being pet owners at our admittedly advancing ages. We talked about the advantages of being able to come and go as we pleased without worrying about a dog's needs, pet sitters, and other associated issues. After much reflection, however, I realized that it is *essential* for me to have another dog.

I am mainly an introvert. I'm a homebody who has a few close friends with whom I like to go out and do things. Quite frankly though, I'm content to be at home in the company of my dog and Stu.

I also believe in my heart that Wimsey would give us her blessing. She knew how much we loved her, and I know she would want us to be happy, even if that means sharing our lives with another dog, one that will give us pleasure but will never be her "replacement" because there can never be a replacement for Wimsey.

After further discussion, Stu and I agreed to adopt a dog when the time was "right." We agreed that we didn't want to train another puppy, deal with housebreaking, teething, and other "baby" issues. We also decided that, as much as we loved our English cocker spaniel, we wouldn't bring another one into our lives. We didn't want to risk comparing the new dog to Wimsey. So, we agreed to "retire" her breed from our consideration.

I started to search for a "young" smaller dog of either gender, one that is spayed or neutered, and housebroken. I looked at rescue sites in Arizona and California and was narrowing our search to full-bred or mixed breed Maltese, Havanese, Bichon Frisé, and Lhasa Apso.

We agreed to actively search for our new dog starting in May 2020, just after our granddaughter's third birthday celebration in Fresno. We also agreed on our current life priorities of focusing on our physical and emotional health and well-being, spending time with our family, and when the time comes, sharing our lives with a new furry friend. We recognized that bonding with our future dog, to have him or her feel at home and understand our expectations, would take time and patience. We also planned to continue traveling but were willing to slow the pace to accommodate our future fur baby.

Now, here comes the interesting part...

While having lunch with my friend Tracy in early February 2020, she asked how we were doing after losing Wimsey. I shared my sadness with her. She asked if we would ever get another dog. I told her that we are contemplating adopting a smaller, housebroken, young companion dog, and added that we prefer a spayed female but would consider a neutered male. She asked about our preferred breed and I said that I was most interested in a Maltese or a Maltese mix.

Tracy responded that her boyfriend Wil has three dogs: a male Maltese, a female terrier, and one of their offspring, a young Maltese-mix female terrier. She said Wil wants to downsize his brood and is interested in finding a good home for his two-year-old female.

She called Wil from the restaurant and, as luck would have it, he was at home. She explained my interest in adopting a young Maltese-mix female dog. Shortly after Tracy and I finished our lunch we met up again at Wil's home where we were enthusiastically greeted by Frodo, the Maltese male, his partner Nilla (the color of a vanilla wafer), and the spunky Maggie, aka Magnolia. We had a wonderful visit in his yard. I was happy to finally meet Wil and to learn what a nice guy he is. And I got a chance to observe Wil and Tracy interact with his three pups and saw how well they all played together.

Wil explained his interest in finding a good home for Maggie ("Three dogs are one too many," he said.) and his unwillingness to place a notice for her on Craigslist or some other site. I held Maggie on my lap as she anointed me with doggy kisses before bouncing off to join her parents as they chased a squirrel up a tree. I told Wil

I was interested in Maggie but added that I wanted Stu to meet her before committing. Wil said he was in no hurry to rehome Maggie and assured me that our time constraint was not an issue for him.

The whole experience felt like a dream!

I sent Stu a lengthy text message along with a few photos. Within two minutes, Stu called and said, "Let Wil know we're interested in adopting Maggie." He said that my assessment of Wil and Maggie were good enough for him. He already knew and liked Tracy.

After further discussion, Stu followed up with a text message to Wil, which he promptly answered. There were more text messages back and forth and more positive messages. We were both sold!

At our first opportunity, we took a marathon 22-hour drive to and from Fresno in mid-March and drove home with our new 13-pound bundle of traumatized anxiety.

We planned to spend the remainder of 2020 acclimating Maggie to our home, teaching her new rules and acceptable behaviors, and developing relationships with our new furry friend. We introduced Maggie to a new vet and new toys. She has also been exposed to new sights, scents, and sounds like those from the loud ducks and geese living in our backyard lake.

Sadly, Maggie's traumatic anxiety never ceased and in fact grew worse. She developed a pathological attachment to me and experienced severe separation anxiety when I was out of her line of vision for more than twenty minutes. She howled, jumped over a forty-inch gate on several occasions, and hurled herself against a door. She soiled our office and chewed our woodwork. But she was in the worst misery when I had to leave our home for a medical appointment or even to clean the garage. We took videotapes to show a behavioral veterinarian specialist. The vet prescribed four different psychopharmacological medications and numerous behavioral exercises, all intended to ease her anxiety. Nothing worked.

Much to our dismay, our very sweet, lovable dog could not find peace except when she was near me. The veterinarian said we'd never be able to leave her and that she could never be cured. She told us Maggie's chances for a successful rehoming were essentially nonexistent because of the severity of her attachment disorder. It was not the vision we had of our life with Maggie. We were devastated.

Another part of our springtime 2020 reality occurred when I took a really freaky fall at Starbucks that resulted in a fractured right hand and a forever-bent ring finger, probably due to severed tendons.

But mainly, we can't forget the world's unwanted and uninvited guest: the coronavirus, aka COVID-19. Sitting here at my desk in Arizona in quarantine, I contemplate our collective fate as we all sit tethered to our televisions, iPads, and computer screens in an attempt to separate truth from fiction. How many people will die? How many will live, post-infection, with comorbid diseases? How many businesses will survive? What will this do to our economy? To our government? To our lives?

We deserve to hear credible information from infectious disease experts unlike the lies, spin and self-serving promotions we heard from Trump and his task force, all vying to maintain their political power. We are left to wonder what the likely impact of this virus will be, with our clear lack of testing supplies, undersupply of personal protective equipment, and the growing necessity to venture out of our homes to obtain consumer goods.

Only recently have effective vaccines become available, albeit on a limited basis. The infection and death curves ebb and flow, while new strains of the mutated COVID-19 virus emerge from other parts of the world. Meanwhile, Trump devotees continue to flout public health guidelines, slow the transition of our government, and wage war on our Democracy, all in the name of convoluted right-wing conspiracy theories.

In the face of this pandemic, the very least of our concerns is whether there will even be a high school reunion for Bowen's Class of 1970. Due to the pandemic, two previously scheduled reunion dates have been canceled. At present, we don't know when we'll meet again.

I truly hope to see some former classmates in the coming years, preferably in a much-healed environment. Until then, I send my fondest wishes to former Manorites, Southsiders, and Bowenites, with whom I share so many memories. Stay well!

About the Author

Debra (Debbie) Kaplan Low earned a bachelor's degree in journalism and a master's degree in communications from the University of Illinois at Urbana-Champaign. Debbie and Stuart moved to Arizona in 1979 when Stu joined the Arizona State University (ASU) faculty as an assistant professor in the Department of Economics. For several years, Debbie held a dual position as an adjunct faculty member in the College of Business at ASU in both the Marketing Department and in Health Services Administration where she taught marketing communications and health care marketing classes and conducted research on hospice services in Arizona. She has coauthored scholarly articles in academic journals based on findings from this research, as well as case studies later published in marketing and management textbooks.

Debbie went on to earn master's degrees from ASU in Health Services Administration in the College of Business, and in Counseling Psychology. She retired in 2014 from private practice psychotherapy after specializing in adult and couples therapy, with special interests in bipolar disorders, personality disorders and neuropsychology. Previously, she was a medical/health care consultant in Arizona for almost 20 years. In that capacity, she provided management and marketing consulting services to hospitals, medical groups, and tertiary care facilities throughout Arizona. She also published articles in *Arizona Medicine* and other professional journals related to medical management issues.

In Arizona, Debbie has served on the boards of directors of East Valley Hospice, Samaritan Hospice, Hospice of the Valley, the Area Agency on Aging, and Save the Family Foundation of Arizona. She has also written two children's books that await publication.

Debbie and Stu are the parents of Dr. David Low, a tenured associate professor of education at California State University, Fresno. David, his wife Katie, their daughter Ellie, and a newborn daughter, Lexie, live in Fresno.

BIBLIOGRAPHY

Becoming: Michelle Obama. 2018. Crown Publishing, a division of Random House LLC, New York

Between the World and Me: Ta-Nehisi Coates. 2015. Spiegel & Grau, an imprint of Random House, a division of Penguin Random House LLC, New York.

Housing Discrimination in Chicago 1900s–1950s: Rhonda Nara Edwards. June 25, 2017. Africana Studies, Chicago Series, Political Science

How to be An Antiracist: Ibram X. Kendi. 2019. One World, Random House Books. New York.

In the Garden of Beasts: Love, Terror, and An American Family in Hitler's Berlin: Erik Larson. 2011. Crown Publishing Group, a division of Random House Publishing, New York.

Nina's Smile: Terry Cremin. 2018. CreateSpace Independent Platform, North Charleston, SC.

Oxford Textbook of Psychopathology: Theodore Millon, Paul H. Blaney and Roger D. Davis. 1999. Oxford University Press, New York.

The South Side: A Portrait of Chicago and American Segregation: Natalie Y. Moore. 2016. St. Martin's Press, New York.

The Warmth of Other Suns: The Epic Story of America's Great Migration: Isabel Wilkerson. 2010. Random House, New York.

White Fragility: Why It's So Hard for White People to Talk About Racism: Robin DiAngelo. 2018. Beacon Press, Boston.